BETWEEN TEACHER AND TEXT
Rick Ayers and Herbert Kohl, Series Editors

"You Won't Remember Me"

The Schoolboys of Barbiana Speak to Today

Marvin Hoffman

Teachers College, Columbia University
New York and London

Published by Teachers College Press, 1234 Amsterdam Avenue, New York, NY 10027. Published by arrangement with Random House, an imprint of Random House Publishing Group, a division of Random House, Inc.

Library of Congress Cataloging-in-Publication Data

Hoffman, Marvin, 1939–
    "You won't remember me" : the schoolboys of Barbiana speak to today / Marvin Hoffman.
        p. cm. — (Between teacher and text)
    Contains a translation of: Lettera a una professoressa
    Includes bibliographical references and index.
    ISBN 978-0-8077-4814-5 (pbk. : alk. paper) — ISBN 978-0-8077-4815-2 (hardcover : alk. paper)
    1. Lettera a una professoressa. 2. Education, Rural—Italy—Barbiana.
3. Schoolboys—Italy—Barbiana—Correspondence. 4. Educational equalization. I. Lettera a una professoressa. English. Selections. II. Title.
    LC5148.I82B3753 2007
    370.945' 51—dc22
                                                                                    2007013219

ISBN: 978-0-8077-4814-5 (paper)
ISBN: 978-0-8077-4815-2 (hardcover)

Printed on acid-free paper
Manufactured in the United States of America

Mississippi was the crucible in which my earliest understandings of the issues addressed by the Schoolboys of Barbiana were forged. This book is dedicated to all the people who played a part in that awakening: my students at Tougaloo College; the parents, teachers, and children of the Child Development Group of Mississippi; the lifelong friends who entered my life there—John and Lucia Mudd, Lew and Hilary Feldstein, Dorian Bowman, Rockwell Gray, Marian Wright Edelman; my late mentor in all things social and political, Ernst Borinski; my student and friend Arverna Adams, who during her life embodied the dignity and pride that the Schoolboys and Father Milani would have celebrated; and, of course, my wife, Rosellen, dear friend and critic, with whom I've been on this journey from the beginning.

Contents

LETTER TO A TEACHER BY THE SCHOOLBOYS OF BARBIANA: THE ORIGINAL TEXT

Series Foreword

Creative work does not spring forth fully formed from the effort of a single individual. It is always built on the previous work of others, on their efforts, mistakes, insights, and struggles. This holds as much for education as it does for music, dance, theater, physics, and mathematics. This series is an attempt to connect present educators with their predecessors through imaginary dialogs and personal narratives. It is a way of showing the minds of current educators at work at the same time as providing a personal way to enter the history of educational thinking and practice. The goal of the series is to illustrate to teachers and people who want to become teachers that there are living traditions that are transformed by current practitioners. Hopefully it can provide creative connections that will encourage teachers to consider themselves intellectuals and historians, and reaffirm the importance of the teacher as a creative force in the making of education.

The series is also meant to encourage educators to become actively engaged with ideas—not merely with techniques, methods, and strategies but with thinking about children, learning, and the place of education in creating a decent world. Thinking about education and reading past works in the field should not merely be a necessity imposed by taking classes at teacher education institutions. It should be a part of one's life as a teacher and hopefully some of these books will provide models of entering into a continuing and creative dialog with some of the most inspiring and challenging writing about learning and schooling.

I have asked a number of educators to choose a person whose work has been important to them and enter into dialog with that work and by extension with that person. I have also asked them to choose an excerpt from that text which has moved them. Each volume in this series has an essay by a current educator and a selection from the text they are reflecting on. In this way the hope is that you can get a flavor of the original as well as a feel for how it helps shape current thinking.

Paulo Freire, the Brazilian educator, often talked about "reading the word and reading the world." For him reading in both contexts implies entering into dialog. In the case of a text this dialogic reading consists, among other things, of questioning the text, relating it to one's active moral, political, philosophical and personal concerns. It can involve doubting the text, incorporating it into one's thinking or action, rewriting it for current times, fantasizing the author answering questions raised about it, and wrestling to give it current significance. It is an active, participatory experience that makes a text come alive in the present.

The books in this series are an attempt to do just this—to show the life in a text through its current transformations. The essays are not critical analyses of the texts, exposition of their ideas, or accounts of their historical or educational importance. Rather they are explorations of the texts and the lives of the authors, acts of discovery that can lead to new ways of thinking through current problems through the wisdom of past educational insights.

Marvin Hoffman got his start in education in the American South, when civil rights struggles and teaching were deeply intertwined. In 1970, the arrival of the translation of the Schoolboys of Barbiana book contributed to his growing commitment to the practice of education as social justice work. Following 3 years as Director of Teachers and Writers Collaborative in New York, Marv moved to Vermont with his wife, the novelist Rosellen Brown, and taught in a small rural school—an experience he described in his book, *Vermont Diary*. He remained in New England for 9 more years, during which he directed the innovative teacher education program at Antioch New England and served as teaching principal in a New Hampshire mill town. Before moving to Chicago he worked in the Houston public schools, developing teachers while continuing to teach middle school and high school students. This work is recounted in his second book, *Chasing Hellhounds*.

Currently, Marv is the Founding Director of the North Kenwood Oakland Charter School in Chicago and Associate Director of the Urban Teacher Education Program at the University of Chicago. His continued relationship with this subversive project in a poor district of Tuscany, and his work to uncover and bring the story to us today, is a moving example of the conversation and practice of liberation between continents and across generations.

—*Herbert Kohl and Rick Ayers*, Series Editors

Acknowledgments

I am enormously indebted to Father James Turnstead Burtchaell, formerly of the University of Notre Dame, who in his book *A Just War No Longer Exists* did much of the biographical work on Don Lorenzo Milani that I used in my introduction. He also brought to the attention of English-speaking readers Father Milani's extraordinary antiwar writings, which the University of Notre Dame Press has been kind enough to grant us permission to reproduce.

The filmmaker Bernard Kleindeinst, who created *Farewell Barbiana* for French television, further deepened my respect for the work at Barbiana by miraculously discovering archival footage from the school and, even more miraculously, tracking down some of the students whose lives are a living monument to Father Milani's passionate commitment.

As further proof of the principle of six degrees of separation, I discovered after I had embarked on this project that Tom Cole, one of the original translators of *Letter to a Teacher*, is the cousin of my son-in-law, Peter Cole. Tom's elegant email exchanges with me about how the book came to be offered insights that even the luckiest of researchers could never hope to be privy to. I can't thank Tom enough, both for the existence of the original book and for his role in its rebirth.

Preface: On Writing

This is how the book came to be.

Don Lorenzo Milani was, among many things, a consummate teacher of writing. His students at Barbiana, public school dropouts from Tuscan peasant families, learned from him the principles of good writing and applied them to great effect in assembling this book.

> Have something important to say, something useful to everyone or at least to many. Know for whom you are writing. Gather all useful materials. Find a logical pattern with which to develop the theme. Eliminate every useless word. Eliminate every word not used in the spoken language. . . . (*Letter to a Teacher by the Schoolboys of Barbiana*, 1970, p. 13, hereafter referred to as *Letter*)

He taught them to compile their notes, place them on individual cards, organize the cards into categories, create sequences for those categories, and fashion titles for each of the sections. They put his advice to good use as they composed their searing indictment of class bias in Italian schools and, by extension, of the entire fabric of Italian society.

I have tried to follow these wise and sensible rules in writing my introductory remarks, so that the final product will at least have the appearance of being cut from the same cloth as the boys' work. But I am one and they were eight.

When I tell friends about my excitement about reviving the Schoolboys' words, I find myself reading to them this passage about good writing, even before I address the Schoolboys' powerful social message. From the moment I discovered the Modern Library Classics in my neighborhood public library in Brooklyn, I have been drawn to the potency of the written word. It is hardly an accident that I married a writer, whose poetry was a draw equal to her beauty, and raised one daughter who is an elegant, professional writer.

Although writing has always taken a backseat to teaching in the way I define myself, I have written two books rooted in my teaching life. More important, I have spent a good portion of that teaching life bringing writers and children together, as well as writing myself with students and their teachers, trying to awaken in them a passion for words and their power to bring clarity and understanding about the world into which they have been delivered. "I don't know what I think until I see what I say," declared the novelist E. M. Forster. Not just think, but feel, I would add. There is nothing so delicious as a classroom full of students communing with their own inner musings and transferring them to paper, away from the nattering voice of the teacher, which so often forces those rich thoughts and feelings and fantasies underground. Absent that moment, the opportunity for private contemplation may never recur as the rest of their lives closes in around them.

My files are bursting with examples of what children are capable of producing in those luminous moments. One of my proudest possessions is a leather-bound volume of my students' writing presented to me by their parents as I was about to move on from a Houston middle school to a new teaching position after 6 years. A thousand moments of young wisdom and fancy captured in amber.

So I thrill to the picture of the Schoolboys around the outdoor table in the courtyard of the church, its belfry surrounded by pencil-thin cypresses that are unmistakable markers of an Italian landscape, arguing about language, sequence, purpose. That image makes me jealous of their fellowship, but, alone, I will try to be faithful to the quality of their work as I tell the story of this book, the man who inspired it, the role it has played in my life, and its significance for teachers today.

Letter
to an
American
Teacher

CHAPTER 1

The Boys

Above all, I want to pay tribute to the boys. They were the sons of Tuscan peasants and poor laborers who had dropped out, or been pushed out, of the Italian school system that, until 1962, required attendance only through fifth grade. Father Milani, a radical priest who had been exiled to this remote village, convinced their parents to entrust them to him to be educated, rather than sending them off to a level of work from which they would never escape.

Father Milani drove them, inspired them, perhaps intimidated them at times, but it is they who ultimately took on the challenge of writing this book, which grew out of a challenge Don Lorenzo posed to address directly those teachers who had failed so badly in the duty to educate them. In addition, the boys devoted themselves to teaching their young counterparts in the school. By age 15 they were seasoned teachers, accomplished writers, professional researchers, and firebrands for justice. Although their writing skills were impressive, to say the least, in the end these were merely a means to give voice to their outrage at the inequities that threatened to deprive them of dignity and opportunity.

The words of these Italian peasant boys, written in the 1960s, resonate with what I learned in Mississippi in the same decade and, sadly, still speak to our struggles in urban America nearly a half century later. They pose for us profound and enduring issues: the purposes of education, the insidious effects of race and class, the capacity to rise above them when students are equipped with an understanding of the forces that have relegated them to an almost inevitable failure to thrive. The Schoolboys and their contemporary counterparts have much to teach us on these subjects, if only we can learn to listen.

LETTER TO A TEACHER

I like to envision the moment when Don Lorenzo hit upon the idea that became this book. Why not set the boys—this was still, sadly, an era when the educational limitations placed on girls remained a given, even with otherwise radical and progressive thinkers—the task of writing a letter to a composite teacher representing all those who had served these children of peasants poorly, had failed them and propelled them right out of the educational system. On their side, the eight voices would merge into one, so that the net effect would be of a personal conversation of which we hear only one side. No question that it's unfair for the embattled teacher to be voiceless in this exchange, but it is small compensation for the years of shy silence endured by these children who had few verbal defenses before Don Lorenzo took them in hand.

After all, the Schoolboys, under Father Milani's leadership, were engaged in nothing less than a war. All they had in their arsenal was the pen, but that would have to suffice to put an end to "the Slaughter of the Poor" (*Letter*, 1970, p. 6), as they labeled the efforts to exile them from the classroom and send them back to the fields. Not to go quietly was a battle for their humanity because, in their view, "ignorance means being shut out of the whole human enterprise."

THE LETTER WE DREAM OF

Every teacher dreams of receiving letters from her former charges, testimonials to the life-changing moments they experienced at their mentor's feet. But in this case the Professoressa to whom the epistle was addressed is the target of a blistering bill of particulars detailing the many ways in which she failed these boys while creating the illusion that the failure was theirs. The anger against this embodiment of all the evils of the educational system runs so deep, the tone so vituperative, that at one point she is equated with a Nazi functionary. Her inadequate efforts on their behalf led them to propose a life of celibacy, which would enable her to devote herself fully to her students without the distractions of family. It is only at the end of their epistolary journey that they are able to step back from their caustic attack, as they imagine receiving a letter that begins:

Dear Boys,
    Not all teachers are like that lady of yours. Don't become racists yourselves. . . .
They know firsthand of the existence of a different breed of teacher because they have been blessed to sit at the feet of the anti-Professoressa, someone who "gives to a boy everything the teacher himself believes, loves, and hopes for. The boy, growing up, will add something of his own and this is the way humanity moves forward." (*Letter*, 1970, p. 134)

The letter that all of us who teach covet is one that I've been fortunate enough to receive a few times from several among the thousands of students who have served their time with me. We cling to the illusion that each one represents hundreds that would have arrived had it not been for the distractions of busy lives. In this book the dreamed-of letter is directed to Father Milani. It is there between the lines of the attack on the Professoressa; Father Milani is everything she is not and the evidence of his success is present in every luminous and incisive word the Schoolboys have composed.

THE OTHER LETTER

Equally impressive is the letter that is spoken by Don Lorenzo's former students, now grown, on a video that surfaced in the course of my research (Kleindeinst, 1994). First we see the school as it was, the boys trudging up the steep, forbidding hill, bundled against the region's rain and cold. We see them gathered around long tables in the presbytery during the winter months, the older boys instructing the younger children. There is even a sprinkling of girls present, although the older group is all boys, who demonstrate a surprising commitment to feminism in their recognition of this gender gap.

> None of the girls from town ever come to Barbiana. . . . Perhaps because of their parents' mentality. They believed that a woman can live her life with the brains of a hen. . . . This, too, is racism. But on this matter we cannot blame you, the teachers. You put a higher value on your girl students than their parents do. (*Letter*, 1970, p. 9)

In spring and summer they move the tables outside under those cypresses, where they write, tinker with an astrolabe that they will use to study the nighttime sky, or sit listening attentively to one of the many fascinating visitors whom Father Milani has invited to make the outside world a reality to children living in what was then a remote corner of Tuscany. Current readers will have to project themselves back in time, to before the international gentrification of the region, to be able to accept that "remote" and "Tuscany" do not constitute an oxymoron.

It is in this outdoor setting where we also see Father Milani, seated in his comfortable rocker, reading the daily paper to his students, who tell us that this activity occupied 1 to 3 hours of each day and was a major component of the focused instruction the priest had substituted for the state curriculum, which he dismissed as useless—"just dates." Through this daily reading, Father Milani brought the larger world—Vietnam, the Cuban missile crisis, coups in Africa—to the inhabitants of a village that was without electricity until 1965. In Don Lorenzo's words, "I couldn't define someone as a rightful sovereign citizen if he can't understand the first page of a paper or the tone of a political program or rally" (Kleindeinst, 1994).

THE BOYS SPEAK

It is the boys themselves, in the film now grown to men, who bear witness to the extraordinary crucible through which they passed under the guidance of Father Milani. They arrived as dropouts, exam failers, retainees, transfers from schools that served them poorly. They bear witness to his belief that they must learn to both write well and speak well. In the words of one student, "It was a weapon that would later enable us to defend ourselves against the bosses, against the doctor's son, against the ruling classes" (Kleindeinst, 1994). The boys call that generic doctor's son Pierino, and into his persona they pack all the unearned privilege, the entitlement from which they are excluded. Against him they juxtapose Gianni, one of their own—a school dropout so damaged that even their radical school could not save him.

There is no need for the teacher to waste her efforts on teaching Pierino to write well because his parents send him to school with those skills already in place. "You say that little Pierino, daddy's boy, can write well. But of course he speaks as you do. He is part of the firm" (*Letter*, 1970, p. 12). The Giannis must struggle to attain what comes naturally to Pierino because their mentor has convinced them that "that man is an equal who can express himself and can understand the words of others" (p. 90).

The Schoolboys' articulate reflections are quarried with enormous effort from the hard rock of their limited lives. "At Barbiana, you had to study, study hard, study well, seven days a week because us country boys had to make up for lost time. Culturally we were centuries behind" (Kleindeinst, 1994). One former student tells of being accepted into the school on a Saturday afternoon after a meeting between the priest and his parents. As the boy left, he told Don Lorenzo he would see him on Monday morning. "No," said the priest, "tomorrow" (Kleindeinst, 1994). At Barbiana, school was in session 12 hours a day, 363 days a year.

The Schoolboys echoed Don Lorenzo's belief that "school, with today's [abbreviated] schedule, is a war against the poor" (*Letter*, 1970, p. 83), who could not afford the extracurricular enrichments available to the higher classes and who had so much to catch up with. The KIPP Academies, a national network of charter schools, now numbering more than 50, are unwitting American descendants of Barbiana. Their students spend 67% more hours in school than their counterparts in most American public schools. Amistad Academy in New Haven and its offshoots in New York City and North Star Academy in Newark are also proponents of a demanding academic regimen aimed at overcoming the daunting gap between low- and middle-income children entering school, which grows ever larger as the years tick by. In the words of KIPP's founders, "There are no shortcuts."

The sons of peasants and laborers are filmed against bookshelf-lined backdrops, behind imposing desks, in tasteful galleries, hunched over drafting tables. They have morphed into teachers, nurses, union leaders, surveyors, art printers, luxury hotel managers, station masters. The positions they find themselves in were unimaginable to the parents who entrusted them to Don Lorenzo. Theirs was a world where white shirts and uncalloused hands were the exclusive domain of those doctors' sons.

Whether the positions the sons of Barbiana find themselves in today are entirely attributable to their time under the priest's tutelage is impossible to say with certainty. The rising tide of the Italian economy over the decades may have lifted all boats. Yet there seems to be something qualitatively different in these boys' ascent. They continue to be reflective about whether the choices they have made are congruent with the elevated ideals the priest instilled in them. They continue to ask questions, as he insisted they do with every outside visitor he brought them. For the most part they comport themselves as graduates of what they call in their text the "School of Social Service," rather than the "School of Ego Service."

Above all, they have found ways to live their lives free of the need for blind obedience to authority. This was the leitmotif of Don Lorenzo's own life, one that he promoted in both word and deed. The students recall a momentous visit to Barbiana from the Cardinal who had been responsible for exiling Father Milani to this place where he refused to languish. Even when the priest kissed his superior's ring, he was able to do it with respect but without submission. This is the balance the priest sought for his students, and in one of the frequent paradoxes we encounter in the educational world—like John Dewey droning on endlessly about the importance of learning by doing—he pursued that goal in a most authoritarian manner.

So the boys, now grown men, through their eloquent filmed testimony, have spoken the letter to a teacher that is the antithesis of the barbed words they aimed at the unfortunate, but not blameless, Professoressa. It is a thank you note, decades overdue, to a man who would have disdained such thanks and, in fact, would have been quick to point out the ways in which they had fallen short of the impossibly lofty goals he had set for them. It is likely that he would have chastised some of them for betraying their working-class origins by adopting the trappings of a middle-class existence. Many of us with roots in the working class know firsthand how wrenching it is to find ourselves enjoying the very successes our parents and teachers prepared us for, wished for us, yet feeling somehow that lurking behind that success lies a betrayal, a distancing from the values that fueled our successes. The Schoolboys must check themselves against the warning they issued many decades earlier, that whatever successes they achieved, could not come at the cost of losing their class identity. In the words they address to one of their own who aspires to become a Pierino, "By a hair I missed becoming one of you, like those children of the poor who change their race when they go up to the university" (*Letter*, 1970, p. 128).

Merely achieving individual success would constitute failure. "To come out alone is stinginess," the boys say (*Letter*, 1970, p. 8). Relentless idealist that he was, Father Milani undoubtedly would have confronted his former charges with evidence—however unfairly presented—of the ways in which they had veered from the path he envisioned for them. True teachers like Don Lorenzo are like the uncompromising Biblical prophets, ever exhorting their people to aspire to a higher standard.

CHAPTER 2

The Priest

MILANI BEFORE BARBIANA

Lorenzo Milani was born between the wars in 1923 and grew up in a polarized time when the political landscape was sharply divided between the fascism of Mussolini and the communism of a large segment of the Italian people. His father was a well-to-do rural landowner and his mother, who outlived him, came from a Jewish background. After a brief stint in art school, one that seems to have left little imprint on his pedagogy, he completed his studies for the priesthood in 1947.

His first assignment was to a parish in Prato, an industrial town near Florence, where his work organizing evening classes for young factory workers presaged his later mission in Barbiana. Despite his popularity among the young workers, his outspokenness and his unorthodox style drew fire from many clerics and, after 7 years, earned him exile to Barbiana, where he would spend the rest of his life. Like many men and women of deep conviction, he was not easy to get along with. He was quick to insult those who did not share his views, or who did not enact them with sufficient zeal, a sure recipe for repeated conflicts with authority and peers alike.

WAR

I have an Italian friend who married an American woman and tried to put down roots in this country. But he was an ardent communist and he wearied of explaining to those he met in the United States that communism in Italy represented a widely held set of political convictions, not the criminal act Americans believed it to be. On a recent visit he made to the United States, I asked him if he had ever heard of Father Milani. "Of course," he said, "everyone in Italy knows about him." My friend is prone to hyperbole; he might have been closer to the truth if he had said that almost everybody of an earlier generation knows about him, which should come as no surprise since Father Milani has been dead now for 40 years.

But what surprised me was that the context in which my friend and, presumably, his peers knew about Don Lorenzo had far less to do with his work at the school than with another issue entirely. In 1965 a group of retired military chaplains published a letter in *La Nazione* denouncing those who refused service in the Italian army on the grounds that they were conscientious objectors. The chaplains declared:

> As for what some call "conscientious objection," the chaplains consider it to be an insult to the fatherland and to its Fallen, as something alien to the Christian commandment of love and as an expression of cowardice. (Burtchaell, 1988, p. 17)

With the support of his students, Father Milani composed a brilliantly argued rejoinder that he circulated among local clergy and sent to many newspapers and periodicals around the country. The only one that published it in its entirety was *La Rinascita*, a communist journal edited, perhaps not coincidentally, by Luca Pavolini, a childhood friend of Milani's.

In his letter, Father Milani stressed one of the central themes of his work at the school—the evils of blind obedience. After leading his readers through a scholarly summary of all the unjust wars in Italy's past, he chastises the chaplains.

> [W]ith history books in hand you should have educated our soldiers for objection, rather than for obedience. . . . The same military obedience that you chaplains glorify without a single *distinguo* to relate it to St. Peter's question: "Is it God or men that we ought to obey?" (Burtchaell, 1988, pp. 21, 27)

The position Father Milani espouses was echoed in Martin Luther King, Jr.'s arguments about our right and responsibility to engage in civil disobedience when confronted with unjust laws. (It is no accident that a simple portrait of Gandhi hung on the wall of Barbiana's presbytery, representing a moral legacy the priest shared with Dr. King.) Like King, Milani recognized that the act of refusal could lead to jail and the willingness to accept such consequences could hardly be seen as cowardice.

We also see in Father Milani's letter the strong class focus that pervades his work, which we will return to further on. The word *fatherland* in the chaplains' original letter triggered a passionate outburst that confirmed the beliefs of his critics that there was more Marx than Jesus in his teachings.

> If you persist in claiming the right to divide the world between Italians and foreigners, then I must say to you that, in your view of things, I have no Fatherland. I would then want the right to divide the world into disinherited

and oppressed on one side, and privileged and oppressors on the other. . . .
And if, without being disciplined by the church, you have the right to teach
that it can be a moral thing—even heroic—for Italians and foreigners to tear
each other to pieces, I claim the right to say that then the poor can and should
take up arms against the rich. . . . The arms which you condone are horrible
devices of war to kill, to mutilate, to destroy, to make widows and orphans.
The only weapons I condone are noble and bloodless: the strike and the ballot. (Burtchaell, 1988, p. 19)

A GLOBAL PERSPECTIVE

At the school Don Lorenzo worked to free his students of the narrow
loyalties to nation, which he saw at the root of all wars. By insisting that
they all break out of their confining Tuscan world and travel throughout
Europe and North Africa, he was certain they would come to see all they
shared with the factory worker in Manchester or the Algerian farmer.

These were not the cushioned adventures of today's middle-class college students spending their semester abroad in Mali or Seville. The Schoolboys were expected to make their way without benefit of a parent's credit
card or cash allowance. They worked as they went, traveled as cheaply as
they could, and reported back to their classmates on the people they met
and the lessons they learned. Samples of those letters, replete with obscure political references of the time, are included in their book because
they were the ultimate evidence of how well their educations had equipped
them to be the fully sentient citizens of the world Father Milani hoped he
was grooming. "In our school, the experience of going abroad takes the
place of your exams. We test our culture by sifting it through life" (*Letter*,
1970, p. 95). The boys were enacting a version of the Native American
practice of sending their young men out into the larger world—in their
case, the larger world of nature—to demonstrate that they were ready to
become full adult members of the tribe.

WAR COMES TO SCHOOL

It should hardly be surprising that these braided issues of war and
class became part of the school's "curriculum." The boys were astonished
by the national attention the case brought to their dying village as Father Milani and his publisher were tried on charges of "incitement to the
crime of desertion and the crime of military disobedience" (Burtchaell,
1988, p. 49). All the discussion generated by the case made them feel

less "marginalized" in relation to the outside world, while at the same time, closer to home, it forced them to confront critical moral issues in their own lives. Some of the boys were old enough to be eligible for conscription and debated with the priest about whether they should refuse. Ever unpredictable, his advice to one boy was to submit, but to refuse to obey any orders that were at odds with the dictates of his own conscience. The boy complied but was sent home after a short stay, presumably more trouble than he was worth, as Don Lorenzo might have anticipated.

THE END ARRIVES

As early as 1960, Father Milani had been diagnosed with a blood disorder that later became leukemia. In typical fashion, he dealt with the bad news by announcing the facts to his students and setting them to research the details of the disease. Although his illness affected him greatly, there is little evidence of any diminution of energy in the video, where we see a large, robust man with bold, attractive features, and a hairline that had been rolled back, like lawn turf, to the middle of his scalp, striding about the hilltop arm in arm with his students. But by 1965, when the trial began, he was no longer able even to travel to Rome to appear in his own behalf. Instead he submitted letters of defense to be read at the trial, which resulted in an acquittal on the grounds that Don Lorenzo and his publisher co-defendant simply were exercising their rights of free speech.

However, the acquittal was overturned by an appeals court in 1967. The publication of the letter had "inflicted damage upon the public order, and . . . it is in the interest of the state to repress any activity which has been found to subvert the people's readiness to observe the law" (Burtchaell, 1988, p. 107). Subverting blind obedience was exactly what Father Milani had in mind. He would have nodded in agreement with this part of the court's ruling, but by the time it was issued he was dead and his name had been removed from the case. His death came just weeks after the original Italian edition of *Lettera a una Professoressa* was published in 1967 to the kind of acclaim that would have both pleased and discomfited him.

He is buried in the small walled graveyard of Barbiana. The video shows some of his beloved boys carrying his casket to its final resting place, while a large crowd of shirt-sleeved friends, students, and admirers looks on.

The school did not last much beyond his death. The boys tried to keep it going for a time, instructing the little ones as they had in the past, but like so many ventures born out of the passion of one visionary and sustained by his charisma, Barbiana was a shell without Don Lorenzo. So the boys decided to shut it down. Other charismatic figures, as far back as Tolstoy, created experiments to educate the poor, only to abandon them as their lives and interests moved on. For Don Lorenzo, it was life that abandoned him and cut short a commitment that surely would have consumed him to the end of however many years he had been allotted.

CHAPTER 3

The Times

TIMELINES

I have always been fascinated by the timelines one finds in colorful illustrated history books, which show what was occurring simultaneously in different parts of the world while momentous events were unfolding on the West's narrowly defined center stage. In 1492, while Columbus arrived in the New World and the Jews were being expelled from Spain, what was happening in the kingdoms of Africa or in the vast reaches of China?

When *Lettera a una Professoressa* was published and while Father Milani lay dying in Barbiana, my wife and I were in Mississippi celebrating the birth of our first daughter. We were coming to the end of a 3-year stay in the heart of segregationist America. We had come south to teach in an historically Black college, many of whose students came from backgrounds as humble as those of the children of Barbiana. Although the students and faculty had to face physical dangers unknown to the priest and his charges—random shootings, being followed both by police and by anonymous tormentors, attempts to cripple their cars by pouring sugar in their gas tanks—the actual work of educating students continued down a path far more traditional than the one Don Lorenzo chose. Students registered for courses, crammed for exams, accumulated credits, received degrees.

One of the things that was sadly lacking in this environment was an engagement with the question of the very purpose of education. There was an urgency about equipping students to rise out of the desperate poverty that characterized most of their communities, but what then? The poverty that Don Lorenzo encountered in Barbiana was no less grinding than that of the Mississippi Delta, but he was able to see beyond the next rise and ask what kinds of people education should be aspiring to produce and what kind of world they should be equipped to fashion. "We are searching for a goal. It must be an honest one. A great one. It must demand of a boy that he be nothing less than a human being." Or, to create students who are able "to understand others and to make [themselves]

14

understood" (*Letter*, 1970, p. 88). This is a very different enterprise from one that aims to produce capable accountants or competent graduate students. And it is certainly different from the myopic standards by which we are asked to measure our successes as educators today.

It was dissatisfaction with the constraints, academic and social, imposed by the timidity of the college that led me to leave for a job with the Child Development Group of Mississippi, the earliest and largest statewide Head Start program in the country. Many of the staff were former civil rights workers, given to a boldness of thought and action not evident on campus. Our education program was aimed as much at the parents of our preschoolers as at the children themselves. Long deprived of their rights as citizens, they were being encouraged to register to vote, to participate in literacy classes, to apply for government programs that were their right, and to assume direct responsibility for managing the institutions that served their children. For children to move ahead, parents had to take the first step.

Father Milani and his Schoolboys understood from the beginning that parents had to play a critical role in demanding for their children the education they deserved. The parents had to become outspoken about refusing to accept "Right from the start, a poorer school for the poor" (*Letter*, 1970, p. 4). The parent who was content to allow the teacher to blame the victim ("I guess we just weren't blessed with an intelligent boy") (*Letter*, 1970, p. 27) had to be supplanted by the father in our book who, having heard that there was a school in Barbiana that might provide his son with a proper education, proceeded to purchase him a flashlight so he could make the walk safely from his distant village in the early morning hours. In the video, we meet a mother, now elderly, who stands with the interviewer on a windy hilltop looking down on Barbiana in the distance as she describes cutting a path with her scythe from home to school so that her son would not have to arrive with his clothes soaked after a trek through the tall wet grass. Everywhere I have worked—in Mississippi, New Hampshire, New York, Texas, Chicago—there are parents like these who are prepared to be advocates for their children against formidable obstacles.

Out of the corner of my eye, I also was beginning to look at the children during my visits to the Head Start centers. The educators on our staff—at this point I did not consider myself one of them—were creating stimulating environments filled with colorful materials and the kind of conversation usually absent in the unadorned, rough wood cabins that were their homes. These valiant efforts to bring high-quality instruction to the children most in need of it often were thwarted by the rude circumstances of their lives. Children weak with anemia laid their heads on tables covered with drawing materials and blocks, too fatigued to appreciate them. But those Mississippi parents and I were getting our first glimpse of what good education actually looked like, a preview that would serve all of us well in the future.

DOLCI

In Italy, as in America, this was a time of great social ferment. At the same time that Father Milani was enacting his own concoction of Marxist Gandhian Christianity, in the south Danilo Dolci was organizing Sicilian peasants, inhabitants of Italy's Mississippi, to stand against the Mafia, whose stranglehold relegated them to permanent poverty. Although his name is now as unfamiliar to most Americans as Milani's, at the time Dolci was embraced by the American left, which raised money to support his work, traveled to Sicily to stand by his side, and even conspired to have him nominated for the Nobel Peace Prize. As it happens, one group of his supporters, based at MIT, included Tom Cole and Nora Rossi, who, in the course of their involvement with Dolci, learned of the work in Barbiana and were responsible for its translation and publication in this country.

POVERTY AND WAR

During that same period, my wife and I joined a group of protestors on the steps of the post office in Jackson, Mississippi, opposing the war in Vietnam. For most Mississippians, support of civil rights and opposition to the war were cut from the same bolt of communist fabric, and the scorn that they directed at us as they passed those steps was a palpable reflection of that belief.

It was 1967, the year *Lettera a una Professoressa* was published in Italy, the year of the final trial of the conscientious objection case, and the year of Father Milani's death. It was also the year in which Martin Luther King, Jr. delivered his now famous speech—a year to the day before his assassination—in opposition to the war in Vietnam, a speech that brought him criticism even from many of his most ardent supporters and allies, who were made nervous by linking the War on Poverty and the war being waged thousands of miles away.

> [M]any persons have questioned me about the wisdom of my path. At the heart of their concerns, this query has often loomed large and loud: Why are you speaking about war, Dr. King?. . . Peace and civil rights don't mix, they say. Are you hurting the cause of your people, they ask? And when I hear

them, though I often understand the source of their concern, I am nevertheless greatly saddened, for such questions mean that the inquirers have not really known me, my commitment, or my calling. Indeed their questions suggest that they do not know the world in which they live.

With a few small word changes, this is a speech Father Milani would have been proud to deliver, but by the time these words were spoken, he had already been dead a month.

TURBULENT TIMES

I speak of my own situation during this time, not because it was unique in its circumstances or significance, but precisely because it was shared by many others in one form or another and, most particularly, by a group of activists whose primary commitment to education was born in this period. The sit-ins began the same year I started graduate school, followed by the all-too-familiar procession of demonstrations, assassinations, marches, and murders that were the medium in which the beliefs, commitments, and passions of my generation grew, along with our suspicions, our anger, and our distrust of authority. It was the double whammy of the war and the civil rights struggle that shaped our work with children and infused it with its special bittersweet flavor.

CHAPTER 4

The Canon

Out of these times of political and social turmoil, both national and international, a new canon of socially conscious, activist educational literature was emerging. In 1967 Herb Kohl published *36 Children*, an account of his teaching experiences in Harlem classrooms. In particular, Kohl focused on a single year during which his life became intertwined with his students', liberating from them a flood of writing of which few readers would have imagined them capable. Yet, watching the lives of many of them unravel after they left his classroom, Kohl asked a question fraught with potential despair: Is one good year enough? If the answer is no, then our work as teachers is in vain.

Still, many socially conscious young people, including men who had chosen to teach as a way to avoid being drafted to serve in that contemptible war, were drawn to Kohl's vision of the impact a dedicated teacher could have on the lives of desperately needy children, even in the face of an intransigent school system and all the social forces that created the undertow that threatened to pull them back down to the bottom. We agonized over this same question in Mississippi, wondering whether the effects of that good preschool year could survive the battering of the grim, still segregated public school years ahead. These words of the Schoolboys seemed tailor made for those young teachers. "To get to know the children of the poor and to love politics are one and the same thing. You cannot love human beings who were marked by unjust laws and not work for better laws" (*Letter*, 1970, p. 87).

When I returned from Mississippi, I became director of a program that Kohl had begun called Teachers and Writers Collaborative, which sought to build on his discovery of what good writing opportunities could unleash from within formerly voiceless children. An early partner of Teachers and Writers Collaborative was a group called the Voice of the Children, founded by a teacher, Terri Bush, and June Jordan, who already was solidifying her reputation as one of the most imposing Black poets of her generation. Together they met and wrote regularly with a group of Black children in Brooklyn. Their work resulted in a much-admired volume of writings by the children, which bore the name of their group. Like so much of the work that followed, it was a cry of anguish at the violence, filth, and despair that characterized their neighborhoods. These were important new voices but they contained within them a risk of generating a kind of impotent voyeurism on the part of their audience, which was the antithesis of the result Father Milani wanted the Schoolboys' voices to produce. During this same period, Stephen M. Joseph edited a collection of urban student writing called *The Me Nobody Knows* (1969), which later was adapted into a Broadway musical. The suffering of some had become others' entertainment.

It's hard to imagine the hard-edged writing from Barbiana becoming the stuff of song and dance. The emergence of these new children's voices set the context for my reading of the Barbiana Schoolboys' writing. As was the case with Tolstoy's peasant children at Yasnaya Polyana, our children wrote primarily from their imaginations; Father Milani found little use for the imagination in the harsh lives of his children. Writing was utilitarian, a tool for changing their lives, their families, their class. Milani, the former art student, found scant value in any of the arts for his students. The same was true for sports or any manifestation of popular culture, all of which he saw as time-wasting distractions from the monumental catch-up task that confronted his students.

I suspect the priest would have found himself in league with today's educators who have eliminated recess to make room for more instructional time. It is clear from the interviews with his grown students that, as appreciative as they were for what he had given them, there was at the same time sadness over their lost childhoods and their lack of access to other means of self-expression. They were not fully convinced that "nothing but politics can fill the life of a man today" (*Letter*, 1970, p. 72), as he had taught them to believe.

But Barbiana was not yet part of the American landscape. Jonathan Kozol, in *Death at an Early Age* (1967), uttered a cry of rage against the Boston schools where he taught long enough to witness the stifling of young Black spirits. Many readers will remember his account of facing disciplinary action because he read with his students Langston Hughes's poem "The Ballad of the Landlord," about the relation between oppressor and oppressed. For Kozol it was the beginning of a crusade of outrage that peaked with *Savage Inequalities* (1991) and continued through *Shame of the Nation* (2005), an indictment of the resegregation of American schools. His appearances continue to draw large crowds of young people moved by his troubling message and eagerly seeking ways they can help to right the wrongs of American society.

There were others whose books on friends' bookshelves were sure to catch the prepared eye: George Dennison's forgotten gem, *The Lives of*

Children (1969/1999), an account of the small storefront community school on New York's Lower East Side where he and his wife-to-be served children who had been cast aside by the school system as too troubled to educate; the eccentric aristocrat Ned O'Gorman's tale of his labor of love in another storefront, this one in Harlem, named after Addie Mae Collins, one of the victims of the Birmingham church bombing, aptly titled *The Storefront* (1970); Allen Graubard's *Free the Children* (1972), an account of the innovations and excesses of the schools created by young teachers that were as much retreats from the politics of the time as attempts to engage them. In *Utopian Essays and Practical Proposals* (1962), the radical philosopher Paul Goodman, whose primary interest was not education, nonetheless put forth the idea that schools should be brought closer to the people by situating small schools within residential units like public housing high rises. Bill Ayers, whose work entered the radical educators' canon much later, ran a preschool in Ann Arbor during this period, but his involvement in the Weather Underground, which led to 11 years in hiding, delayed bringing those experiences into print. In an innovative project called Foxfire, Eliot Wigginton mobilized his otherwise disengaged students to explore the culture of their North Carolina hills through interviews with local residents who were the repositories of the area's history and culture. These were published at first in a modest magazine, which later became part of a virtual empire of books, videos, and even a local museum that was the home for their discoveries. In the very end of their book, the Schoolboys express their longing for such a curriculum that recognizes and honors what they come from. "Our culture is a gift we bring to you. A vital breath of air to relieve the dryness of your books written by men who have done nothing but read books" (*Letter*, 1970, p. 109).

Both John Holt, an iconic figure among the young dissident teachers of the time, and Robert Coles, whose award-winning trilogy, *Children of Crisis* (1964), gave voice to the children of the segregated south, the hollows of Appalachia, and the isolated Indian reservations, contributed moving postscripts to the Barbiana book when it appeared in translation in 1970.

THE CANON GOES INTERNATIONAL

The publication of Joseph Featherstone's *Schools Where Children Learn* (1971) broadened the horizons of the educators who were looking critically at how to make American education more effective, both pedagogically and politically. Featherstone described the innovative work with public school children in Leicestershire and other parts of England. In these "open classrooms," children were engaged in exploration rather than passive learning. It was the embodiment of Dewey's beliefs in learning by doing. They worked in groups, untethered from their isolated desks. They engaged with materials as well as texts.

Like many other attractive but loosely defined educational reforms, the open classroom concept meant different things to different people. In some places it became a physical concept—the creation of school buildings without full walls separating classrooms. In others it was reflected in the reluctance of teachers to exercise authority in their own classrooms. Neither of these interpretations was remotely related to the original ideas of the Leicestershire teachers. Much of the broad impact of the open classroom concept fell under the heading of what Donald Graves once labeled in a talk "When Bad Things Happen to Good Ideas." There was little visible political or social context to these changes, although one could argue that the encouragement of exploration and the questioning that ensued from that process contained implicit challenges to authority and passive obedience. Once freed from those desks, children were in a position to claim a much more active role in the management of their own learning.

ENTER BARBIANA

Letter to a Teacher by the Schoolboys of Barbiana was published in the United States in 1970, after having achieved great acclaim in Italy 3 years earlier. I can't recall my first reading of it, or how I came upon it, but its significance was instantly clear to me. Someone outside America was struggling openly and explicitly with making education an instrument to combat the inequities of the social and political system. I knew nothing of Father Milani and my knowledge of how this book came to be was limited to what I found in the brief introduction to the English translation by Nora Rossi and Tom Cole. These remote Italian villagers knew all about Stokely Carmichael (*Letter*, 1970, p. 70), but I knew nothing of them.

This book came into my life just as I was edging toward becoming a classroom teacher myself, a role my training as a clinical psychologist hardly had prepared me for. The voices of those boys, so articulate and so appropriately angry at the system that had given up on them and relegated them to the discard pile of social failure, mingled with the voices of the children in Mississippi, Harlem, Appalachia, and the Lower East Side. They suggested that there were ways to continue the work of the waning civil rights movement, to harness the angry energy of war protest, and to fashion a work life that was true to the values the civil rights activists and antiwar protestors lived by. We were so fearful of "selling out," as had so many on the left in previous generations, or so it seemed to us. Here was a way to live a "normal" life that was at the same time purposeful and uncompromised. One of my favorite teacher-authors, James Herndon, once said, "If you only work to change things, you will simply go nuts" (Herndon, 1971, p. 14). In the course of making revolution, it was best to be sure you were having fun along the way, since there was a fair chance that nothing more would come of it. Working with children promised to be fun—most of the time.

Letter to a Teacher had particular resonance for me because, to use a word that was not part of the 1970s lexicon, it sought to empower children by helping them acquire the means for self-expression—writing and speaking. Whoever had performed the magic that enabled the Schoolboys of Barbiana to have their say in ways that were devoid of ventriloquism, set the gold standard for this work. But when the book first appeared, there were the predictable doubters who were incapable of believing that boys of such humble backgrounds could produce such searing prose. The first publisher to whom the translation was offered questioned the book's authorship, angering all who were involved in the project. Fortunately, Jason Epstein, then editor-in-chief at Random House, accepted the book on faith, even without knowledge of the intense grilling the translators had endured at the hands of the Schoolboys themselves about the value of authorizing the publication in America and England.

The young authors' achievement stands as a reminder of what children are capable of, given a strong sense of purpose and access to the tools to accomplish that purpose. It is the same lesson that Jaime Escalante's students in *Stand and Deliver* (1988) taught their detractors who thought them incapable of mastering the intricacies of calculus.

My best efforts over the years at encouraging students to give voice to their ideas and feelings seem timid by comparison. Even the fine work by more recent heirs of the early activist reformers—Stephen O'Connor, Greg Michie, and the founding editors of the magazine *Rethinking Schools*, who have elicited words full of beauty and anger from their students—has not managed to produce the kind of sustained and meticulously argued, all-encompassing vision of their condition that can match that of the Schoolboys.

CHAPTER 5

The Elephant in the Room

As I was following the wise guidelines for writing by which Father Milani had trained his students, I made an interesting discovery. The largest pile of my index cards clustered under the word *class*. This would come as no surprise to the Schoolboys, whose class identities lay at the very center of their being. It was the identity to which Don Lorenzo exhorted them to remain faithful. So why is it that we seem to tiptoe around class in our own discussions of our most pressing social issues? We have no such reservations about acknowledging the role of race at the heart of our problems. It calls to mind our post-Freudian willingness to speak frankly about sex, but to remain more secretive and circumspect about discussing money.

What is there about class that causes such discomfort in our society? The upper class eschews class labels to avoid calling undue attention to itself. Public figures who refer to class are immediately accused of fomenting divisiveness. Acknowledging the existence of class interests and class differences is seen as tantamount to a call for armed revolution. Even the members of what others would recognize as the lower or working class have an aversion to those labels for fear that admitting to such an identity would foreclose on their ability to transcend it. Our collective identity hovers around the all-encompassing middle class, either in aspiration or attainments, and the insidious effects of class membership go unacknowledged and unremedied.

I was recently in a New England statehouse on the day a bill was being signed to make trusts perpetual (in most states they expire after several generations), thereby cementing the privileges of class for eternity. Many people of greatest wealth in the state were present to celebrate the devious path that had brought this legislation into being, but few of them would declare themselves unashamedly as upper class. This tacit agreement between those at both ends of the class spectrum to maintain silence about their positions and the accompanying unbridgeable differences is one reason revolution and class conflict are almost unimaginable in American society.

Although the teachers-turned-teacher-educators mentioned above come from diverse backgrounds, they are united by a deep recognition of the importance of class in understanding both the causes and possible remedies for what ails our schools. World views ranging from socialist to radical inform their school politics. They understand that, although there is no denying the overwhelming significance of race in understanding the inequities of American society, that fact must not obscure the singular role played by class as well, even within minority communities. As I write this, today's *Chicago Tribune* includes excerpts from letters by middle-class Black readers expressing dismay and disappointment at the gap that exists between the classes in the Black community. I live in one of the few communities on the South Side of Chicago that is integrated, but the nature of that integration is reflected in the cynical motto, often recited facetiously by local residents, "Black and White together, united against the poor." Even here, there is a tendency not to use the word "class" to identify people. The preference is for euphemisms like low income, disadvantaged, economically challenged; "poor" is about as daring as it gets.

The precipitous decline of traditional labor unions in this country has further eroded class identity. My father was a garment worker, a loyal member of Local 119 of the International Ladies' Garment Workers' Union. He had lived through the struggles to create that union and was proud of his membership in it. He may have had middle-class aspirations for his son, but although he didn't use the term, he was unabashedly working class, aware of the gap that lay between him and his bosses. The owners of Dubrowsky and Joseph: Fine Coats for Women lived a life of expensive educations, large suburban homes, and out-of-town colleges for their children that were beyond my father's reach and contrary to his sense of who he was.

That class consciousness he passed on to me. Although, like so many children of immigrants, I have become middle class in work, interests, and tastes, my class identity remains strong, particularly when I am in the presence of privilege. A raw anger rises in me at the injustice of people living with an unearned sense of entitlement, while others struggle, often with little success, to claw their way up out of the deep hole to which society has relegated them. A few of my young teachers-to-be share with me a class history that produces anger in the face of inequity as a natural by-product. I am equally impressed by those who seem capable of seeing beyond their own privilege to arrive at a similar, no less genuine, anger.

GIANNI AND PIERINO

The Schoolboys were certain of where they stood in the class hierarchy. By positing the characters of Gianni and Pierino, they gave a face to the class distinctions that were so glaringly evident in their society. Pierino was the doctor's son, born with the silver spoon in his mouth. The schools were designed to suit him and rigged to ensure that the privilege his father's position had bestowed upon him would be preserved into the next generation. In the same way, the system ensured that Gianni, like his peasant father, would not rise above his starting position. From the day he entered school, it was conspiring to force him out. The kind of work it asked of him, the constraints it imposed on him, were alien and were intended to underscore his own inadequacy, to dampen his aspirations.

We have seen that the Schoolboys are capable of what their translators call "racism," which seems to connote a kind of nasty and barbed stereotyping. Pierino is one of their victims. He is a composite whipping boy, someone they have never met. Gianni and his kind, on the other hand, they encounter daily. They are able to acknowledge what a challenge these difficult boys are, yet how important it is for schools to rise to that challenge.

> We too soon found out how hard it is to run a school with them around. At times the temptation to get rid of them is strong. But if we lose them, school is no longer school. It is a hospital which tends to the healthy and rejects the sick. It becomes a device to strengthen the existing differences to a point of no return. (*Letter*, 1970, p. 13)

Although Gianni arrives at that point of no return and drops out, unsuited at this point even for Father Milani's school, his classmates grant him the honor of having the last word by showing him their manuscript so that he can testify to the truth of their account.

> He finally came. He read it. He pointed out some words or phrases that were too difficult. He reminded us of some tasty bits of viciousness. He authorized us to make fun of him. He is practically the chief author. (p. 133)

AN AMERICAN GIANNI

In his classic *Lives on the Boundary*, Mike Rose (1990) has documented from his own working-class past the oppressively low expectations of the children and families of his community. There was nothing beyond the horizon to aspire to, no sense of how to get there—if there was a there to get to. The networks of social capital that provide the nourishing medium in which middle- and upper-class children swim do not exist for our Mike Roses, our Giannis. When questions of college attendance arise—if children have managed to survive in school that long—they are not privy to college tours, test prep classes, information exchange about the benefits of Carleton over Macalester, Hampshire over Sara Lawrence. None of this even begins to capture the countless invisible and insidious ways in which lower- and working-class students are not invited to the party because of the distinctive way their families raise them and the way academic institutions fail to recognize and reflect those differences. Rose's escape from his class origins is almost accidental, the exception that proves the rule, and it is unclear what students like him have sacrificed along the way that Father Milani might have urged them to cling to.

Gianni was not so fortunate, although in mid-20th-century Italy, he still would have been able to scratch out a foothold for himself that is no longer available in the first decade of the 21st century. Postindustrial society on both sides of the ocean no longer has a place for the lower and working classes, but still they do not rise up, paralyzed in part by a lack of the class consciousness that Father Milani felt obligated to instill in his charges.

THE PROBLEMS PERSIST

What you will read here of the Schoolboys' original work is not the complete original. In the 40-plus years that separate us from them, many things have changed. The Italian school system has been restructured in ways that are not especially relevant to our story, apart from the fact that the years of compulsory education have been extended as part of Italy's move away from its agrarian roots. Therefore, the sections of the original book that are specific to the system of that time have been deleted.

The greater loss is in the elimination of the entire final section of the book. This was intended to be a work of the head, as well as the heart. The head was represented by data the students compiled for this section from state records that enabled them to show the extent to which the dropout rate in Italian schools was a function of class. In their acknowledgments, the boys thank ISTAT, the Central Institute for Statistics, for its help in the exhaustive data collection and analysis. For the statistical work they did so well, they were awarded a prize by the Italian Physical Society. Both words and numbers were effective weapons in their hands.

Once again, those numbers reflect a world that has, in large measure, passed, so there is no need for us to pore over them. The loss lies in our being deprived of a chance to see, implicitly, the tools with which Father Milani equipped his students and the power of those tools to uncover, for themselves and others, the narrative of injustice that controls their lives. One can only imagine the excitement the boys must have felt as the patterns emerged from their data, like a photographic image slowly taking shape in the developing tray, and the strength they must have felt in the validation of what their hearts knew all along. The editors of *Rethinking Schools* recently published a volume entitled *Rethinking Mathematics* (Gutstein & Peterson, 2005) that contains numerous examples of activities that demonstrate to students the power of statistics and data to expose inequity.

Should we be surprised that in a different country in a different century, the findings of the Schoolboys about the links between class on the one hand and high school and college graduation rates on the other remain true? Recent research by the Consortium on Chicago School Research at the University of Chicago presents us with a direct link to those outdated Italian findings compiled by students far less skilled than the trained statisticians and researchers at the Consortium (Roderick, Nagoaka, & Allensworth, 2006).

The picture painted by the Consortium's findings is a bleak one, and although its focus is exclusively on Chicago, there is no reason to believe that other U.S. cities are faring any better. Despite efforts by the Chicago Public Schools to present the numbers in a more positive light, more than half the students in the system drop out before completing high school. Students in the University of Chicago's Urban Teacher Education Program were treated to a graphic representation of that when we visited a high school on the city's South Side. In the building's lobby were posted students' homeroom assignments. Together they formed a steep slope of failure as the numbers dwindled from freshman through senior years, with the sharpest drop occurring between freshman and sophomore years. For the vast majority of these students there is no Father Milani awaiting them, nothing but the streets and, for too many of them, jail. The Schoolboys say of each of the disappeared students, "At his old desk, there ought to be a cross or a coffin as a reminder" (*Letter*, 1970, p. 35).

The Consortium's work extends this dark tale one step further with a finding that has shocked into a stunned silence almost everyone to whom I have presented it. The researchers followed a group of ninth graders in the Chicago Public Schools, until they reached the age of 25. All the students in this cohort were on target to graduate at their expected time; to this point, none had been left back. At 25, long enough for stragglers to have made it through, only 6.5% of the group had graduated from a 4-year college. (This figure is remarkably similar to the 8.1% of students from among the children beginning first grade in the Schoolboys' study who graduated from college, almost none of whom were from working-class backgrounds.) Members of minority groups fared even worse, African American boys worst of all. Officials of the school system have taken issue with the findings. The data, they contend, were compiled on a group that came through the system in an earlier era, before recent improvements had taken hold. Furthermore, graduation rates were not reported for all colleges. Although allowing for these contentions may raise the numbers a bit, the findings remain deplorable, an indictment no less compelling than the one prepared by the Schoolboys.

It is true that the Consortium's data are not reported directly by social class, but the findings are supported by data linking individual students and the income levels of the census tracts in which their schools are located. There is no question that we are looking, in large part, at evidence of the deep wounds that class has inflicted on our children.

CHAPTER 6

Barbiana Speaks to Today

FAST FORWARD

In the years immediately after the book's publication, I directed a teacher education program in rural New England, preparing idealistic young people, many of them recently returned from tours in the Peace Corps, to work in rural schools serving low-income White students. Together we studied the messages from Barbiana to inspire us in our work in the mill towns and farming communities of New Hampshire and Vermont. Like most books that excite me, *Letter to a Teacher* disappeared from my shelf with regularity. I pressed it on people in the heat of conversation and failed to record the identity of its new, and therefore permanent, owner.

In the decades since the 1970s the book faded from my consciousness, and in that I was not alone. Overt political and social agendas in education were less intense in those years, with the exception of some reactive responses to the growth of the testing juggernaut, the resulting rigidification of curriculum, and the stranglehold of large school bureaucracies. The protest and confrontation years of the 1960s and early 1970s had both energized and debilitated the activist community. The narcotic effect of Reagan, the Great Communicator, managed to lull even working-class Americans into ignoring their own interests. At the same time the softening influence of the domestic life into which many activists like me entered, as we married and began to grow our own families, put more confrontational action on hold. Our generation was spawned on America's racial battles and the fight against unjust wars abroad. We were blessed with the good fortune of living at the intersection of our personal trajectories and such monumental historical forces; those who followed were deprived of such clear and defining ideals. The struggles for women's rights and for the environment were—and continue to be—of profound significance, but the absence of clear and identifiable villains tended to leave a different stamp on their supporters.

THE WORM TURNS

Yet the seeds of the old educational activism lay dormant through the decades that, although quiet, were not entirely silent, as was evident in the pre-Bush protests against the introduction of numbing assessments and the growth of testing and textbook empires, harbingers of much larger confrontations to come. Among those protesters were the members of the North Dakota Study Group (NDSG), a loose confederation of intrepid progressive educators who came together under the leadership of Vito Perrone, at that time Dean of the University of North Dakota Graduate School of Education and later a revered member of the faculty at Harvard. For almost 40 years NDSG has been the voice of opposition against the rising tide of defining education by the numbers.

The Schoolboys were scathing in their condemnation of testing and in their recognition that it was yet another instrument designed to keep them on the outside looking in. Picture this moment:

> While giving a test you used to walk up and down between the rows of desks and see me in trouble and making mistakes, but you never said a word. . . . And over there, a few steps away, you stand. You know all of these things. You are paid to help me. Instead, you waste your time keeping me under guard as if I were a thief. (p. 122)

Toward the end of the book, we encounter the collective narrator repeatedly knocked to the canvas by the testing system that stands between him and the teaching certificate he covets. "You flunked me again, as if you were spitting on the ground. But I am not going to give up. I will be a teacher and I'll make a better teacher than you." Unfortunately, that system of testing designed to favor the Pierinos had long since sent many of the students who entered first grade with him back to the fields to work alongside their parents.

It is important to note that despite the bitter indictment of testing and the recognition of the differential harm it inflicted on the poor, the vast majority of students in Barbiana passed the state exams year after year. Although Father Milani chose to ignore the state curriculum on which the tests were based, he was a realist about the need to suspend their "real" work for a period each year to prepare students for the exams. Unlike many of the schools serving the poor today that have made test preparation their entire curriculum, at Barbiana those efforts were more circumscribed and never confused with the purposeful learning that retained center stage.

In late 1992, I attended a conference in Washington, D.C., convened by the late Senator Paul Wellstone, who was preparing to become head of the education subcommittee in the Clinton administration about to take office. Wellstone had enlisted Herb Kohl to round up the usual suspects, whose voices had been muted for so long, to advise the new regime on what it could do to put education back on a more humane and equitable course. The participants included the admirable activist teachers who founded the journal *Rethinking Schools* in Milwaukee, government and foundation executives who had come of age within the movement and were now eager to use their new positions of influence to pursue their original goals, and people like me who had hunkered down in our own classrooms hoping the conservative winds would blow themselves out. We appeared to be on the threshold of a new period of hope.

Title I of the Elementary and Secondary Education Act, originally passed in the glory days of the 1960s—1965 to be exact—was up for reauthorization, and the participants saw the installation of the new administration as a rare opportunity to return this potentially powerful piece of legislation to its original goal of reducing the performance gap between low-income children and those in the middle and upper classes. Like so many well-intentioned efforts at top-down social reform, it had been effective for some poor children, while leaving others even more deeply mired in failure. For those, the emphasis of Title I on drill and practice of basic skills had, in fact, widened the gap in thinking and problem-solving skills. Our seeming incapacity to learn from history has led us to the same impasse in the new testing era created by No Child Left Behind following its passage in 2001. The weight of its single-minded emphasis on judging school success on the basis of narrowly conceived testing falls most heavily on the children of the poor whose schools have eschewed the development of rich, engaging curricula of the sort that elevated Father Milani's students, in favor of a numbing test preparation regime.

THE NEXT GENERATION

At the same time that the older generation of educational activists was resurfacing, a whole generation of young people, beneficiaries of a period of enormous economic advances among middle-class and suburban Americans (mostly, although not exclusively, White), was searching for its own defining cause, its own way out of that School of Ego Service so aptly labeled by the Schoolboys of Barbiana. In 1990, Wendy Kopp created Teach for America (TFA), which for more than the past decade and a half has placed many thousands of graduates of prestigious colleges in urban and rural schools throughout the country that serve poor children. Although teaching is often a brief sojourn en route to professional careers in other

areas for the majority of TFA participants, the response it elicits from graduates of highly regarded colleges and universities nonetheless reflects a spirit
similar to that of those early Peace Corps volunteers. They share a belief
that something is amiss in the way resources—intellectual and material—
are distributed and that they own some responsibility to use their own
privilege to contribute to righting that imbalance.

FULL CIRCLE

After more than 30 years in classrooms from kindergarten through
high school, including a 5-year stint as the director of a charter school on
Chicago's South Side serving predominantly low-income African American children, I find myself back where I was in the early 1970s, co-directing
a teacher education program. The goal remains to provide the best possible education for children and families all too accustomed to being short-
changed, although this time the focus has shifted from rural to urban.
The Urban Teacher Education Program (UTEP) prepares graduates of the
University of Chicago to work in challenging schools of the kind that wash
out a shocking number of new teachers who are poorly prepared to face
the enormous social and institutional obstacles those schools present. Pre-
liminary data from the Consortium on Chicago School Research indicate
that as many as 80% of beginning teachers working in high-poverty urban
schools leave within the first 2 years.

The students at the University of Chicago, like so many of their counterparts in TFA, are beneficiaries of a demanding course of study. Their
privileged educations equip them to contemplate many choices that are
more lucrative, more prestigious, and less burdensome than teaching. What
awaits them is a workday as draining as that of an air traffic controller, in
marked contrast to the office life that many of their peers will pursue. They
will be paid inadequately for their efforts and suffer low status and limited respect. Unlike many of their TFA counterparts, they approach teaching as a long-term commitment, one for which they need to be well
prepared for some of the most difficult work they will ever be called upon
to do. Spending time with them and witnessing their tears and their anger,
as they act with determination to overcome the inequities and injustices
that so much of the rest of the society has actively chosen to ignore or
deny, represents nothing less than a rebirth for the activists of my generation, a reassurance that the earlier battles for a more just society have not
been, to use George Orwell's term, vaporized. They are taking root again,
against obstacles that may be even more formidable than the ones my
generation faced earlier. The testing culture is more dominant and perva-

sive. There appears to be less wiggle room, less license to try daring things and, perhaps, to fail. The stakes for their students—possible failure and retention—are too high.

A DIFFERENT USA

Joseph Featherstone speaks of our society as the United States of Amnesia, forever oblivious to the events and lessons of the past. As part of my own small effort to connect past to present, I have introduced the UTEP students to parts of the early canon that shaped me as a teacher. We read *36 Children* and marvel at the amazing work that Kohl's students produced, while acknowledging that even more formidable barriers to working with children in such a creative way have been erected in the ensuing 4 decades.

We read Paulo Freire, whose work, while not rooted in the classroom, provided my generation with a philosophical, political, and sociological basis for understanding the forces standing against us, along with an inspiring story of success in overcoming those obstacles in a landscape strewn with noble failures.

I invited Bill Ayers to join me and the UTEP students in our discussion of Freire's extraordinary efforts to help the desperately impoverished peasants of rural Brazil stand against the forces that silenced them. Our agenda that day included conversation about Maxine Greene, one of Bill's mentors and sources of inspiration at Columbia University's Teachers College. Her concept of "wide awakeness" as a central goal of education is the antithesis of the mind-numbing statistical objectives mandated by No Child Left Behind. It was the reminder the students needed that behind their studies of letter blends and math materials still lay the larger purposes that originally had drawn them to teaching, the desire to prepare students who were fully aware of who they were, where they wanted to go, what the obstacles were to getting there, and how to overcome them.

REACQUAINTANCE

While reading Greene and Freire in preparation for these sessions, I was reminded of my long ago romance with the Schoolboys of Barbiana. The connection between those peasant children of Tuscany and Freire's Brazilian farm workers was evident, but, although I had not thought of the Schoolboys in terms of wide awakeness in my original reading, it now seemed obvious that their clear-eyed analysis of the ongoing battles between the oppressors and the oppressed was the essence of wide awakeness.

When I went in search of a replacement for my long-lost copy, I found that it was out of print, and only with difficulty did I find a used copy through which to resume my acquaintance with the Schoolboys. It was that copy, clothed in the familiar white jacket with red spine and lettering that had stared back at me from my bookshelf for so many years, that I brought to class that day. I had marked several passages to read to the students, including my favorite about what constitutes good writing, although, truth to tell, I wanted to read it to them cover to cover. I had to fight back tears to get through the reading. I felt overwhelmed at once by the power of these children's words speaking across the decades. Judging from the reactions on the faces of the eager young teachers-in-the-making around the seminar table, those words had lost none of their power to move new readers. It was an affirmation in dark times that truth may be muzzled temporarily, but it retains a power that, eventually, will break free and be heard again. It was in that seminar room that I decided to begin working to bring those words back to life, certain that they contained a message that a new generation wanted and needed to hear.

RECONNECTING WITH THE PAST

Perhaps it is no surprise that so many of the educational activists of my generation have, like me, become teacher educators: Bill Ayers at the University of Illinois at Chicago, Herb Kohl until recently at the University of San Francisco, Jay Featherstone at Michigan State, and, most recently, Deborah Meier at New York University. We are the repositories of a history whose disappearance would drain our own lives of meaning. Some of us remained in the schoolhouse longer than others, but we are all of an age where, painful though it may be to admit, voices younger and more energetic than ours are more likely to be attended to by children. The loss of the pleasures of the hurly burly of school life, what I've described elsewhere as "living a novel every day," is tempered by the feeling that, through our work with young teachers, we can stand against the dystopian vision of education currently in the ascendance, which, as a school board member in Houston once said to me, threatens "to destroy children's souls" (Hoffman, 1996, p. ix).

Part of that work involves reconnecting with the educational visions of the past from Plato to Horace Mann to Dewey and beyond. But it also calls for celebrating the rare moments when the victims of the system, who, since the beginning of time, have been either poor or minorities or both, find their voices. The Schoolboys' collective voice, rising from its remote Tuscan corner, needs to be heard again.

AMERICAN SCHOOLBOYS

We need to create the opportunities for our own American Schoolboys to emerge, armed with a strong sense of who they are and equipped with the skills to speak truth to power. Father Milani believed literally in the importance of the ability to speak and write in ways that would force those in charge to hear his students without dismissal. Like the Italian Schoolboys, our American Schoolboys must acquire the technical and mathematical skills to lay bare the real impact of privilege, or the lack of it, on the ability of others like them to succeed.

Against heavy odds, there are places and programs scattered around the country that are working toward this end—the Urban Academy in New York, the Albany Park Theater Project in Chicago, and the Algebra Project in Cambridge, Massachusetts, to name a few. Recently I was part of a design team for a new Chicago high school that, in addition to promoting rigorous academic standards (a cliché these days among new schools, which almost universally present themselves as college preparatory programs), proposed that a major portion of students' upper level work revolve around what we called signature projects. Most of these projects involve students studying closely some aspect of their community, exposing challenges to that community, and proposing action to remedy them. These are the kinds of strong voices Father Milani would have been proud to hear in his own barren corner of Tuscany.

Letter to a Teacher by the Schoolboys of Barbiana:

The Original Text

PART I

The Compulsory Schools Ought Not to Flunk Their Students

Dear Miss,

You won't remember me or my name. You have flunked so many of us.

On the other hand I have often had thoughts about you, and the other teachers, and about that institution which you call "school" and about the kids that you flunk.

You flunk us right out into the fields and factories and there you forget us.

Timidity

Two years ago, when I was in first *magistrale,** you used to make me feel shy.

As a matter of fact, shyness has been with me all my life. As a little boy I used to keep my eyes on the ground. I would creep along the walls in order not to be seen.

At first I thought it was some kind of sickness of mine or maybe of my family. My mother is the kind that gets timid in front of a telegram form. My father listens and notices, but is not a talker.

Later on I thought shyness was a disease of mountain people. The farmers on the flatlands seemed surer of themselves. To say nothing of the workers in town.

Now I have observed that the workers let "daddy's boys" grab all the jobs with responsibility in the political machines, and all the seats in Parliament.

---

*magistrale: A four-year upper school leading to a diploma for elementary school teachers.

So they too are like us. And the shyness of the poor is an older mystery. I myself, in the midst of it, can't explain it. Perhaps it is neither a form of cowardice nor of heroism. It may just be lack of arrogance.

THE MOUNTAIN PEOPLE

The School for All

During the five elementary years the State offered me a second-rate education. Five classes in one room. A fifth of the schooling that was due me.

It is the same system used in America to create the differences between blacks and whites. Right from the start a poorer school for the poor.

Compulsory School

After the five elementary years I had the right to three more years of schooling. In fact, the Constitution says that I had the obligation to go. But there was not yet an intermediate school in Vicchio. To go to Borgo was an undertaking. The few who had tried it had spent a pile of money and then were thrown out as failures like dogs.

In any case, the teacher had told my family that it was better not to waste money on me: "Send him into the fields. He is not made for books."

My father did not reply. He was thinking, "If we lived in Barbiana, he would be made for books."

Barbiana

In Barbiana all the kids were going to school. The priest's school. From early morning until dark, summer and winter. Nobody there was "not made for school."

But we were from a different parish and lived far away. My father was ready to give up. Then he heard of a boy from San Martino who was going to Barbiana. He took courage and went to find out.

The Woods

When he came back I saw that he had bought me a torch for the dark evenings, a canteen for soup, and boots for the snow.

The first day he took me there himself. It took us two hours because we were breaking our path with a sickle and a billhook. Later I learned to make it in little more than an hour.

I would pass by only two houses along the way. Windows broken, recently abandoned. At times I would start running because of a viper or because a crazy man, who lived alone at the Rock, would scream at me from the distance.

I was eleven years old. You would have been scared to death.

You see, we each have our different kind of timidity. So, in that sense we are even.

But we're even only if both of us stay at home. Or if you have to come and give us the exams at our place. But you don't have to do that.

The Tables

Barbiana, when I arrived, did not seem like a school. No teacher, no desk, no blackboard, no benches. Just big tables, around which we studied and also ate.

There was just one copy of each book. The boys would pile up around it. It was hard to notice that one of them was a bit older and was teaching.

The oldest of these teachers was sixteen. The youngest was twelve, and filled me with admiration. I made up my mind from the start that I, too, was going to teach.

The Favorite

Life was hard up there too. Discipline and squabbles until you didn't feel like coming back.

But there a boy who had no background, who was slow or lazy, was made to feel like the favorite. He would be treated the way you teachers treat the best student in the class. It seemed as if the school was meant just for him. Until he could be made to understand, the others would not continue.

Recess

There was no recess. Not even Sunday was a vacation.

None of us was bothered by it because labor would have been worse. But any middle class gentleman who happened to be around would start a fuss on this question.

Once a big professor held forth: "You have never studied pedagogy, Father Milani. Doctor Polianski writes that sports for boys is a physiopsycho. . . ."*

He was talking without looking at us. A university professor of education doesn't have to look at schoolboys. He knows them by heart, the way we know our multiplication tables.

Finally he left, and Lucio, who has thirty-six cows in the barn at home, said, "School will always be better than cow shit."

The Peasants of the World

That sentence can be engraved over the front doors of your schools. Millions of farm boys are ready to subscribe to it. You say that boys hate school and love play. You never asked us peasants. But there are one billion, nine hundred million of us. Six boys out of every ten in the world feel the same as Lucio. About the other four we can't say.

All your culture is built this way. As if you were all the world.

Children as Teachers

The next year I was a teacher; that is, three half-days a week. I taught geography, mathematics and French to the first intermediate.

You don't need a degree to look through an atlas or explain fractions.

If I made some mistakes, that wasn't so bad. It was a relief for the boys. We would work them out together. The hours would go by quietly, without worry and without fear. You don't know how to run a class the way I do.

Polianski: We never heard this name but he must be a famous educator. *Physiopsycho*: The first half a big word used by that professor; we cannot remember the ending.

Politics or Stinginess

Then, too, I was learning so many things while I taught. For instance, that others' problems are like mine. To come out of them together is good politics. To come out alone is stinginess.

I was not vaccinated against stinginess myself. During exams I felt like sending the little ones to hell and studying on my own. I was a boy like your boys, but up at Barbiana I couldn't admit it to myself or to others. I had to be generous even when I didn't feel it.

To you this may seem a small thing. But for your students you do even less. You don't ask anything of them. You just encourage them to push ahead on their own.

THE BOYS FROM TOWN

Warped

When the intermediate school was started in Vicchio, some boys from the town came to Barbiana. Just those who had failed, of course.

The problem of shyness did not seem to exist for them. But they were warped in other ways.

For example, they felt that games and holidays were a right and school a sacrifice. They had never heard that one goes to school to learn, and that to go is a privilege.

The teacher, for them, was on the other side of a barricade and was there to be cheated. They even tried to copy. It took them one hell of a time to believe that there was no grade book.

The Rooster

The same subterfuges when it came to sex. They believed they had to speak in whispers. When they saw a rooster on a hen they would nudge each other as if they had seen adultery in action.

In any case, sex was the only subject that would wake them up at first. We had an anatomy book at school. They would lock themselves up to study it in a corner. Two pages became totally worn out.

Later they discovered other interesting pages. Later still, they noticed that even history is fun.

Some have never stopped discovering. Now they are interested in everything. They teach the younger children and have become like us.

Some others, however, you have succeeded in freezing all over again.

The Girls

None of the girls from town ever came to Barbiana. Perhaps because the road was so dangerous. Perhaps because of their parents' mentality. They believed that a woman can live her life with the brains of a hen. Males don't ask a woman to be intelligent.

This, too, is racism. But on this matter we cannot blame you, the teachers. You put a higher value on your girl students than their parents do.

Sandro and Gianni

Sandro was fifteen; five feet eight in height: a humiliated adult. His teachers had declared him an imbecile. They expected him to repeat the first intermediate year for the third time.

Gianni was fourteen. Inattentive, allergic to reading. His teachers had declared him a delinquent. They were not totally wrong, but that was no excuse for sweeping him out of their way.

Neither of them had any intention of trying yet again. They had reached the point of dropping out and getting jobs. They came over to us because we ignore your failing marks and put each person in the right year for his age.

Sandro was put in the third intermediate class and Gianni in the second. This was the first satisfaction they ever had in their unhappy school careers. Sandro will remember this forever. Gianni remembers once in a while.

Gianni could not be made to put the h on the verb "to have." But he knew many things about the grown up world. About jobs and family relations and the life of his town's people. Sometimes in the evening he would join his dad at the Communist Party meeting or at the town meeting.

You, with your Greeks and your Romans, had made him hate history. But we, going through the Second World War, could hold him for hours without a break.

You wanted him to repeat the geography of Italy for another year. He could have left school without ever having heard of the rest of the world. You would have done him great harm. Even if he only wants to read the newspaper.

"You Can't Even Speak Properly"

Sandro became enthusiastic about everything in a short time. In the morning he devoted hours to the same course he would have studied in the third intermediate year. He would take notes on the things he didn't know and at nights he would poke around in the books of the first and second intermediates. This "imbecile" took your exams at the June session and you had to let him pass.

With Gianni it was harder. He had come to us from your school illiterate and with a hatred of books.

We tried the impossible with him. We succeeded in having him love not every subject; but at least a few. All that we needed from you teachers was to pass him into the third intermediate and to give him lots of praise. We could have taken upon ourselves to make him love the rest.

Instead, a teacher said to him during the oral exam, "Why do you go to private school, boy? You know that you can't even speak properly?"

(_____.)*

We certainly do know that Gianni can't speak properly. Let's all beat our breasts about that. But most of all, you teachers, who had thrown him out of school the year before.

Fine remedies you have.

Without Distinction as to Language

Besides, we should settle what correct language is. Languages are created by the poor, who then go on renewing them

---

*Here should be a word that came to our lips that day, but the publisher refused to print it.

forever. The rich crystallize them in order to put on the spot anybody who speaks in a different way. Or in order to make him fail exams.

You say that little Pierino, daddy's boy, can write well. But of course; he speaks as you do. He is part of the firm.

On the other hand, the language spoken and written by Gianni is the one used by his father. When Gianni was a baby he used to call the radio "rara." And his father would correct him: "It's not called rara, it's called 'aradio.'"

Now, it would be a good thing for Gianni also to learn to say "radio," if at all possible. Your own language could become a convenience in time. But meanwhile, don't throw him out of school.

"All citizens are equal without distinction as to language," says the Constitution, having Gianni in mind.

Obedient Puppet

But you honor grammar more than constitutions. And Gianni never came back, not even to us.

Yet we can't get him off our mind. We follow him from a distance. We heard that he doesn't go to church any more, or to any political meetings. He sweeps up in a factory. During his free time he follows like a puppet whatever is "in." Saturday, dancing; Sunday, the ballpark.

But you, his teacher, don't even remember his existence.

The Hospital

This was our first contact with you. Through the boys you don't want.

We, too, soon found out how much harder it is to run a school with them around. At times the temptation to get rid of them is strong. But if we lose them, school is no longer school. It is a hospital which tends to the healthy and rejects the sick. It becomes just a device to strengthen the existing differences to a point of no return.

And are you ready to take such a position? If not, get them back to school, insist, start from scratch all over again, even if you are called crazy.

Better to be called crazy than to be an instrument of racism.

EXAMS

The Rules of Good Writing

After three years of schooling at Barbiana I took, in June, my exams for the intermediate diploma as a private-school candidate. The composition topic was: "The Railroad Cars Speak."

At Barbiana I had learned that the rules of good writing are:

Have something important to say, something useful to everyone or at least to many. Know for whom you are writing. Gather all useful materials. Find a logical pattern with which to develop the theme. Eliminate every useless word. Eliminate every word not used in the spoken language. Never set time limits.

That is the way my schoolmates and I are writing this letter.

That is the way my pupils will write, I hope, when I am a teacher.

The Knife in Your Hands

But, facing that composition topic, what use could I make of the humble and sound rules of the art of writing in all ages? If I wanted to be honest I should have left the page blank. Or else criticized the theme and whoever had thought it up.

But I was fourteen years old and I came from the mountains. To go to teachers' school I needed the diploma. This piece of paper lay in the hands of five or six persons alien to my life and to everything I loved and knew. Careless people who held the handle of the knife completely in their own grasp.

I tried to write the way you want us to. I can easily believe I was not a success. No doubt there was a better flow to the papers of your own young men, already masters in the production of hot air and warmed-up platitudes.

Social Climbers at Twelve

But your students' own goal is also a mystery. Maybe it is nonexistent; maybe it is just cheap.

Day in and day out they study for marks, for reports and diplomas. Meanwhile they lose interest in all the fine things they are studying. Languages, sciences, history—everything becomes purely grades.

Behind those sheets of paper there is only a desire for personal gain. The diploma means money. Nobody mentions this, but give the bag a good squeeze and that's what comes out.

To be a happy student in your schools you have to be a social climber at the age of twelve.

But few are climbers at twelve. It follows that most of your young people hate school. Your cheap invitation to them deserves no other reaction.

The Parents' Union

Our teacher went around saying he was stuck with a class made up of imbeciles. Who should have kept him in check?

The principal might have been able to do it, or the teachers' council. They did not.

The parents might have been able to do it. But as long as you have the handle of the knife completely in your grasp they will keep quiet. And so, either we have to wrest from your hands all the knives (marks, reports, exams) or we have to get the parents organized.

A wonderful union of fathers and mothers able to remind you that we are the people who pay you; and we pay you to serve us, not throw us out of school.

It may turn into a good thing for you. People who get no criticism do not age well. They lose touch with life and the progression of events. They turn into poor creatures like yourselves.

The Newspaper

The history of this half-century was the one I knew best. Russian Revolution, Fascism, war, resistance, liberation of Africa and Asia. It is the history lived by my father and my grandfather.

I also knew well the history of my own time. That means the daily newspaper, which we always read at Barbiana, aloud, from top to bottom.

While cramming for the exams we would steal a couple of hours every day to read the paper, overcoming our stinginess. Because nothing is found in the newspaper that could help us pass your exams. This proves again how little there is in your school useful for life.

That is why we must read the news. It is like shouting in your face that your filthy certificates have not turned us into beasts. We want the diploma for our parents. But politics and the news of each day—they are the sufferings of others and are worth more than your interests or our own.

The Constitution

One woman teacher ended her lessons before the First World War. She stopped exactly at the spot where school could tie us to life. In the whole year she never once read a newspaper to her class.

The Fascist posters must still be dangling before her eyes: "Do not talk politics in here."

Gianpietro's mother was talking to her one day: "But you know, I feel that my child has improved so much since he started going to the *doposcuola.* * I see him reading at home in the evening."

"Reading? Do you know what he reads? The CONSTITUTION! Last year he worried about girls, this year it's the Constitution."

That poor woman was made to feel that it must be a dirty book. That night she wanted Gianpietro's father to give him a good beating.

Order of Priorities

If schooling has to be so brief, then it should be planned according to the most urgent needs.

Little "Pierino," the doctor's son, has plenty of time to read fables. Not Gianni. He dropped out of your hands at fifteen. He is in a factory. He does not need to know whether it was Jupiter who gave birth to Minerva or vice versa.

His Italian literature course would have done better to include the contract of the metalworkers' union. Did you ever read it, Miss? Aren't you ashamed? It means the life of half a million families.

You keep telling yourselves how well educated you are. But you have all read the same books. Nobody ever asks you anything different.

---

*After-hours school.

Unhappy Children

At the gymnastics exam the teacher threw us a ball and said, "Play basketball." We didn't know how. The teacher looked us over with contempt: "My poor children."

He, too, is one of you. The ability to handle a conventional ritual seemed so vital to him. He told the principal that we had not been given any "physical education" and we should take the exams again in the fall.

Any one of us could climb an oak tree. Once up there we could let go with our hands and chop off a two hundred-pound branch with a hatchet. Then we could drag it through the snow to our mother's doorstep.

I heard of a gentleman in Florence who rides upstairs in his house in an elevator. But then he has bought himself an expensive gadget and pretends to row in it. You would give him an "A" in physical education.

South Africa

Some people hate equality.

A school principal in Florence told a mother: "Don't you worry, madam, send your son to us. Our school is one of the least egalitarian in all of Italy."

It is quite easy to cheat the "sovereign people." One can do it just by starting a special class for the "nice" boys. It is not necessary to know them personally. It's enough to look at their report cards, their age, their address (farm or city), place of birth (North or South), father's profession, and influential references or pull.

In this way, two, three, and even four intermediates will co-exist in the same school. Class A is the "intermediate old-style." The class that runs smoothly. The best teachers will fight to have it.

A certain kind of parent will go to a lot of trouble to have a child placed in it. Class B will not be quite as good, and so on down the line.

The Duty to Push

But these are all honorable people. The principal and the teachers are not doing it for their own good; they are doing it for the good of Culture.

Not even the parents act for their own good. They are acting for the child's future. To push one's own way through is not proper, but to do it for the child's good is a Sacred Duty. They would feel ashamed not to.

Disarmed

The poorest among the parents don't do a thing. They don't even suspect what is going on. Instead, they feel quite moved. In their time, up in the country, they could only finish the third grade.

If things are not going so well, it must be that their child is not cut out for studying. "Even the teacher said so. A real gentleman. He asked me to sit down. He showed me the record book. And a test all covered with red marks. I suppose we just weren't blessed with an intelligent boy. He will go to work in the fields, like us."

STATISTICS

At the National Level

Here you might object that we happened to take our examinations in particularly bad schools. Also, that whatever reports we receive from elsewhere all happen to be sad. You can say that you know a lot of other examples, as true as ours, but leading to the opposite conclusions.

So, let us drop, all of us, a position that has become too emotional, and let us stand on scientific ground.

Let us start all over, this time with numbers. Unfit for studying, Giancarlo took on himself a job of compiling statistics. He is fifteen years old. He is another of those country boys pronounced by you to be unfit for studying.

With us he runs smoothly. He has been engulfed in these figures for four months now. Even math has stopped being dry for him.

The educational miracle we have performed on him comes out of a very clear prescription.

We offered him the chance to study for a noble aim: to feel himself a brother to 1,031,000 who were failed, as he was, and to taste the joy of revenge for himself and for all of them.

Gianni Means Millions

Schools have a single problem. The children they lose. The Giannis.

Your "compulsory school" loses 462,000 children per year. This being the case, the only incompetents in the matter of school are you who lose so many and don't go back to find them. Not we: We find them in the fields and factories and we know them at close range.

Gianni's mother, who doesn't know how to read, can see what the problems of the school are. And so will anybody who knows the pain endured by a child when he fails, and who has enough patience to look through statistics.

Then these figures will begin to scream in your face. They say that the Giannis run into millions and that you are either stupid or evil.

Shooting Into a Bush

To flunk someone is like shooting into a bush. Perhaps you get a boy, perhaps a hare. We'll find out in time.

You don't know what you have done until the following October. Has he gone off to work or will he repeat the year? If he repeats, will he get anything out of it? Will he gain some solid ground for going on with his studies, or will he just grow older badly in courses not made for him?

Priests and Whores

Mothers are no saints. They do not see beyond their own threshold. That is a great defect. But their children live on the same side of the threshold. They are people mothers can never forget.

Teachers, on the other hand, can always find excuses for forgetting. They are only part-time mothers. The missing child has the defect of not being there. At his old desk there ought to be a cross or a coffin, as a reminder.

Instead, a new student sits there. Another watched little character like him. And the teacher is already growing fond of the new one.

Teachers are like priests and whores. They have to fall in love in a hurry with anybody who comes their way. Afterwards there is no time to cry. The world is an immense family. There are so many others to serve.

It is a fine thing to be able to see beyond one's own threshold. But we have to be sure that we ourselves haven't chased a child away from it.

Only a Fraction of Equality

At the end of the five elementary years, eleven children (of the original 32) have already disappeared from the school, and it is their teachers' fault.

"Schools are open to all. All citizens have a right to eight years of school. All citizens are equal." But what about those eleven?

Not one of them is the son of well-to-do parents. The thing is so clear-cut that we can only smile.

BORN DIFFERENT?

The Stupid and the Lazy

You tell us that you fail only the stupid and the lazy.

Then you tell us that God causes the stupid and the lazy to be born in the houses of the poor. But God would never spite the poor in this way. More likely, the spiteful one is you.

A principal of an intermediate school has written: "The Constitution cannot, unfortunately, guarantee to all children the same mental development or the same scholastic aptitude." But he will never admit it about his own child. Will he fail to make him finish the intermediate? Will he send him out to dig in the fields?

Even the rich have difficult offspring. But they push them ahead.

Others' Children

Children born to others do appear stupid at times. Never our own. When we live close to them we realize that they are not stupid. Nor are they lazy. Or, at least, we feel that it might be a question of time, that they may snap out of it, that we must find a remedy.

Then, it is more honest to say that all children are born equal; if, later, they are not equal, it is our fault and we have to find the remedy.

Removing of Obstacles

This is exactly what the Constitution says, in reference to Gianni:

"All citizens are equal before the law, without distinction as to race, language or personal and social conditions. It is the duty of the Republic to remove the obstacles created by economic and social conditions which, limiting the freedom and equality of citizens, prevent the full development of the human personality and the full participation of all workers in the political, economic and social organization of the country" (Article 3).

IT WAS UP TO YOU

Unloader of Barrels

One of your colleagues (a sweet young bride who managed to fail ten out of twenty-eight children in the intermediate class—both she and her husband Communists, and quite militant) used this argument with us: "I did not chase them away, I just failed them. If their parents don't see to it that they return, that's their worry."

Gianni's Father

But Gianni's father went to work as a blacksmith at age twelve and did not even finish the fourth year level of schooling.

When he was nineteen he joined the Partisans. He did not quite grasp what he was doing. But he understood far better than any of you. He was looking forward to a world with more justice, where Gianni at least could be equal to all. Gianni, who was not even born.

This is the way Article 3 sounds in his ears: "It is the duty of Mrs. Spadolini [a teacher] to remove all obstacles . . ."

And he pays you, too—quite well. He gets 300 lire per hour, and out of it he pays you 4,300.

Substitution

But Gianni's father cannot by himself remove the obstacles that weigh him down. He has no idea how to discipline a boy going through the intermediate years: how long the boy should sit at his desk, or whether it is good for him to have some distractions. Is it true that studying causes headaches and that his eyes "begin to trill," as Gianni says?

If Gianni's father knew how to manage everything by himself, he would not have to send Gianni to you for schooling. It is up to you to supply Gianni with both education and training. They are two faces of the same problem.

If you lead him forward, Gianni will be able to work with you in a different way and still be a more competent father tomorrow. But for today, Gianni's father is what he is. What he was allowed by the rich to be.

Tutoring

That poor man—if he knew what was going on he would pick up his weapon and be a Partisan again. There are teachers who tutor for money in their free time. So, instead of removing the obstacles they work to deepen the differences among students.

In the morning—during regular school hours—we pay them to give the same schooling to all. Later on in the day they get money from richer people to school their young gentlemen differently. Then, in June, at our expense, they preside at the trial and judge the differences.

The Little Civil Servant

If some little civil servant did his paperwork quickly and well at home, for a good price, but at his desk did the same job slowly and badly, you would have him locked up.

Consider further that should he whisper to clients, "In this office your documents will be given to you late and all messed up. Let me suggest that you find someone who can do them better at home for a little extra," he would be locked up.

But no one locks up that teacher whom I heard say to a mother: "The boy's not going to make it on his own. Get him a tutor." That's what he said, word for word. I have witnesses. I could bring him to court.

To court? To see a judge whose wife herself makes a bit extra by tutoring? Anyway, the Italian Penal Code, for some reason, does not list such a crime.

Onions

You are all in perfect agreement. You want us crushed. Go ahead, do it, but at least don't pretend to be honest. Big deal, to be honest when the Code is written by you and cut to your measurements.

An old friend of mine stole forty onions from a vegetable garden. He got thirteen months in jail, no clemency. The judge of course does not steal onions. Too much trouble. He asks the maid to buy them for him. The cash to pay for both the onions and the maid is made by his wife, with her tutoring.

Freedom

The other obstacle that you make no effort to remove is the sway of fashion.

One day Gianni told us, while talking about TV, "They keep feeding us this junk. If they led us to school instead, that's where we would go."

In town, all kinds of fads press down on him, never anything worthwhile. When a boy doesn't follow the fads, he's "out." Or he needs the kind of courage that Gianni doesn't have—so young, so untaught, and with nobody to help him.

As if our natural desires in themselves didn't give us enough trouble.

Fashions

A fashionable theory holds that the years from twelve to twenty-one are for playing at sports and playing at sex, and for hating studies.

The years from twelve to fifteen are the best ones for mastering the language. And ages fifteen to twenty-one are the best for putting the language to use at union or political meetings. But these facts have been concealed from Gianni.

It has been hidden from him, too, that there is no time to lose. At fifteen it's good-bye to school. At twenty-one personal problems close in: engagement, marriage, children, making a living. He will have no time then for meetings, will be afraid to expose himself, and won't be able to give fully of himself outside his home.

The Defenses of the Poor

Only you teachers could have built a defense for the poor against the rule of fashion. The government pays you 800 thousand million lire a year to do so.

But you are such paltry educators, offering 185 days of holiday against 180 of school. And four hours at school against twelve hours out. An idiot of a principal who walks into a class to announce, "The education officer has granted a new holiday on the third of November," hears a shout of joy and allows himself a smug smile.

You have presented the school as a nuisance; how are the children supposed to love it?

Let's All Embrace Each Other

In the town of Borgo the principal has granted the use of a classroom as a dance hall for the boys and girls of the third intermediate year. The Salesiani Order at their parochial school, not to be outdone, organized a masked parade. A teacher I know parades about with the Sports Gazette sticking out of his pocket.

These are men full of understanding for the "needs" of the young. In any case, it's so easy to take the world as it comes. A teacher with the Sports Gazette sticking out of his pocket gets along very well with a laborer-father who also has the Sports Gazette in his pocket, while they talk about a son who carries a ball under his arm or a daughter who spends hours at the hair-dresser.

Then the teacher puts a little mark in the grade book and the laborer's children have to go to work before they have learned to read. But the teacher's children—they will go on with their studies to the last, even if they "don't feel like it" or "don't understand a thing."

SELECTION IS USEFUL TO SOME

Fate or Plan?

Here someone will start blaming it all on fate. To read history as keyed to fate is so restful.

To read it as keyed to politics is more disturbing: Fashions then turn into a well-calculated scheme to assure that the Giannis are left out. The apolitical teacher becomes one of the 411,000 useful idiots armed by their boss with a grade book and report cards. Reserve troops charged with stopping 1,031,000 Giannis a year, just in case the sway of fashion is not sufficient to divert them.

Who Profits?

Let's try to see who profits from schools kept to a minimum number of hours.

Seven hundred and twenty hours per year means about two hours of school per day averaged out over the year. But a boy stays awake another fourteen hours. In well-to-do families these are fourteen hours of cultural improvement.

But to the peasants they are fourteen hours of loneliness and silence, good only for deepening their shyness. To the sons of workers they are fourteen hours at the school of the hidden persuaders.

Summer holidays, in particular, seem virtually designed for the benefit of the rich. Their children go abroad and learn even more than they do in winter. But by the first day of school the poor have forgotten even the little they knew in June. If they have to take any make-up exams they can't afford a tutor to prepare for them. Usually they give up and just don't take the exam. Peasant boys help on the farm during the heavy summer months in order to pay for their keep.

THE MASTER

Does He Exist?

We may seem to be implying the existence of some master who manipulates you. Someone who has cut the schools to measure.

Does he really exist? Is there a handful of men gathered around a table, holding all the strings in their hands: banks, business, political machines, the press, fashions?

We don't know. If we claim this, we feel our book takes on a certain mystery-story tone. If we don't, we seem to play the simpleton. It is like arguing that so many little gears have fallen into place by chance. Out sprang an armored car able to make war all by itself, with no driver.

Pierino's Home

Perhaps the life story of "Pierino" can give us a key. So, let us try to take a loving look at his family.

The doctor and his wife are up there on top of things. They read, they travel, they see friends, they play with their child, they take time to keep close track of him and they even do it well. Their house is full of books and culture. At five I had mastered the shovel; Pierino, the pencil.

One evening, as if the decision has been brought about by the facts themselves, they say half-jokingly, "Why place him in the first grade? Let's put him straight into the second." They send him to take the test without giving it another thought. If he fails, who cares?

But he does not fail. He gets all 9s. Serene joy fills the family, just as it would have mine.

A Special Case

As it began, so it continues, year after year. Pierino is always promoted and he hardly does any studying.

I fight my way through with clenched teeth, and I fail. He also manages to have time for sports, meetings, as well as time for his puberty crisis, his year of the blues and his year of rebellion.

He is less mature at eighteen than I was at twelve. But he keeps going ahead. He will graduate with full honors. He will become a graduate student at no pay.

Working Gratis

Yes, gratis. Who would believe it; graduate students work without salary.

This is not a romantic disregard for material interests; it is a refined system for keeping out the inferior classes without saying it to their face.

Class struggle when carried on by gentlemen is gentlemanly. It offends neither the priests nor the intellectuals reading their *Espresso*.*

Pierino's Mamma

Pierino, then, will become a professor. He will find a wife much like himself. They will produce another Pierino. More of a Pierino than ever.

Thirty thousand such stories every year.

If we consider Pierino's mother in herself, she is no wild beast. She is just a bit selfish. She has simply shut her eyes to the existence of other children, though she has not kept Pierino from meeting other Pierinos. She and her husband are surrounded by other intellectuals. Clearly, they don't want to change.

As to the thirty-one mothers of Pierino's schoolmates, either they don't have time or they don't know any better. They hold jobs, which pay so little that to make ends meet they have to work from childhood to old age and from dawn to night.

But she was able to go to school until she was twenty-four. Besides, she was helped at home by one of those thirty-one other mothers—the mother of some Gianni who neglected her own son while doing the housework for Pierino's mother.

All the free time she gets to pursue her interests—is it a gift from the poor or is it a theft by the rich? Why doesn't she share it?

The Lion's Share

To conclude the subject of Pierino's mamma, she is neither a beast nor is she an innocent. If we add up thousands of small selfish attitudes like hers, we get the total selfishness of a whole class, claiming for itself the lion's share.

It is a class that has not hesitated to unleash Fascism, racism, war, unemployment. If it became necessary to "change

---

*A well-known weekly newspaper considered left of center, and widely read by the intellectuals.

everything so that nothing would change,"* it would not hesitate to embrace Communism.

No one can know the precise mechanism—but when every law seems cut to measure in order to serve Pierino and screw us, we have difficulty believing in chance.

SELECTION HAS REACHED ITS GOAL

At the University

"Daddy's boys" constitute 86.5 percent of the university student body; laborers' sons, 13.5 percent. Of those who get a degree, 91.9 percent are young gentlemen and 8.1 percent are from working-class families.

If the poor would band together at the university, they could make a significant mark. But, no. Instead, they are received like brothers by the rich and soon are rewarded with all their defects.

The final outcome: 100 percent daddy's boys.

In the Political Parties

The men who staff the various political parties, at every level, are solidly university graduates.

The proletarian parties are no different on this issue. Workers' parties don't turn up their noses at daddy's boys. And the daddy's boys, conversely, don't turn up their noses at proletarian parties. As long as they themselves get the prominent positions.

Indeed, it is quite in with the rich to work "with the poor." That is, not so much "with the poor," as "leading the poor."

The Candidates

Politicians prepare the short lists of candidates. They include the names of a few workers, as window dressing, in order to save face. But later on they see to it that university graduates get preference: "Leave it to people who know their way around.

---

*This is a quote from Giuseppi Tomasi di Lampedusa's classic novel *The Leopard* (1958) about a turbulent period in 19th century Italy.

A worker would feel lost wandering in the legislature. Anyway, Dr. X is one of us."

The Legislature

To conclude, the men elected to make the new laws are the same ones who were quite pleased with the old laws. They are the only ones who have never personally lived through the things that ought to be changed, the only ones who should not be working in politics.

University graduates make up 77 percent of Parliament. They are supposed to represent the voters. But voters with university degrees make up 1.8 percent of the population. Workers and union members in Parliament—8.4 percent. Among the voters—51.1 percent. Peasants in Parliament—0.1 percent. Among the voters—28.1 percent.

Black Power

Stokely Carmichael has been in jail twenty-seven times. He declared at his last trial, "There isn't a white man I can trust."

When a young white who had given his entire life to the cause of the blacks cried, "Not a single one, Stokely?" Carmichael turned to the public, stared at his friend, and repeated, "No, not a single one."

If the young white man took offense at what Carmichael said, then Carmichael is right. If he is truly with the blacks, the young white must swallow it, draw aside, and keep on loving. Perhaps Carmichael was waiting for just this moment.

Newspapers of the left and the center have always applauded any publication on the school of Barbiana. After this book, they may join with the right and start hating us. Then it will be clear that that is a party bigger than all other parties: the party of Italian College Graduates, "Partito Italiano Laureati."

FOR WHOSE SAKE ARE YOU TEACHING?

Good Faith

The good faith of teachers is a different matter entirely. You teachers are paid by the government. You have the

children right there in front of you. You have studied your history. You teach it. You should be able to see more clearly.

Of course, you see only selected children. And you got your
culture from books. And the books were written by men in the
Establishment. They are the only ones who can write. But you
should have been able to read between the lines. How can you
possibly say you are acting in good faith?

The Nazis

I try to understand you. You look so civilized. Not a hint of
the criminal in you. Perhaps, though, something of the Nazi
criminal. That super honest, loyal citizen who checked the
number of soap boxes. He would take great care not to make
mistakes in figures (four, less than four), but he does not question whether the soap is made from human fat.

Even More Timid Than I

For whose sake are you doing it? What do you gain by
making school hateful and by throwing the Giannis out into
the streets?

I can show you that you are more timid than I ever was.
Are you afraid of Pierino's parents? Or afraid of your colleagues
in the upper schools? Or the superintendent?

If you are so worried about your career there is a solution:
cheat a little bit on your pupils' tests by correcting a few mistakes while you are walking up and down between the desks.

For the Good Name of the School

Or perhaps you don't fear something so obvious and so
simple. Perhaps you fear your own conscience instead. Then
your conscience is built wrong.

"I would consider promotion of this child injurious to the
good name of the school," wrote a principal in his report. But
who is the school? We are the school. To serve it is to serve us.

For the Good of the Child

"After all, it's for the child's own good. We must not forget
that these pupils stand at the threshold of high school!" pomp-
ously cried the headmaster of a little country school.

It was immediately clear that only three of the thirty children in the class would go on to the upper years: Maria, the daughter of the dry-goods merchant; Anna, the teacher's daughter; and Pierino, of course. But even if more of the children went on, what difference would it make?

That headmaster has forgotten to change the record on his record player. He hasn't yet noticed the growth of the school population. A living reality of 680,000 children in the first year. Most of them poor. The rich, a minority.

It's not a question of a classless school, as he calls it. His is a one-class school, at the service of those who have the money to push ahead.

For Justice

"To pass a bad student is unfair to the good ones," said a sweet little teaching soul.

Why not call Pierino aside to say to him, as Our Lord said in the parable about the vine trimmers [Matthew 20]: "I am passing you, because you have learned. You are twice blessed: you pass, and also you have learned. I am going to pass Gianni to encourage him but he has the misfortune not to have learned."

For Society

Another teacher is convinced that she has a responsibility towards Society. "Today I pass him into the fourteen year olds' class, and tomorrow he turns up as an MD!"

Equality

Career, culture, family, the good name of the school: You are using tiny sets of scales for grading your pupils. They really are petty. Too small to fill the life of a teacher.

Some among you have understood, but cannot find a way out. Always in fear of the sacred word. And yet, there is no choice. Nothing but politics can fill the life of a man of today.

In Africa, in Asia, in Latin America, in southern Italy, in the hills, in the fields, even in the cities, millions of children are waiting to be made equal. Shy, like me; stupid, like Sandro; lazy, like Gianni. The best of humanity.

The Reforms That We Propose

1. Do not fail students.
2. Give a full-time school to children who seem stupid.
3. Give a purpose to the lazy.

1. DO NOT FLUNK

The Turner

A turner at his lathe is not allowed to deliver only those pieces that happen to come out well. Otherwise he wouldn't make the effort to have them all turn out well.

But you, you can get rid of the pieces that you don't like whenever you wish to. So you are happy taking care of those who are bound to be successful for reasons that lie outside the school.

By Piecework

If all of you knew that, by any means possible, you had to move every child ahead in every subject, you would sharpen up your wits to find a way for all of them to function well.

I'd have you paid by piecework. So much for each child who learns one subject. Or, even better, a fine for each child who does not learn a subject.

Then your eyes would always be on Gianni. You would search out in his inattentive stare the intelligence that God has put in him, as in all children. You would fight for the child who needs you most, neglecting the gifted one, as they do in any family. You would wake up at night thinking about him and would try to invent new ways to teach him—ways that would fit his needs. You would go to fetch him from home if he did not show up for class.

You would never give yourself any peace, for the school that lets the Giannis drop out is not fit to be called a school.

You Are the Ones from the Middle Ages

On extreme provocation at our school we even use the rod. Now don't play squeamish. Forget all those pedagogical theories. If you need a whip I can give you one, but throw away that pen lying on top of your record book. That pen leaves its mark all through the year. The mark of a whip disappears by the next day.

Because of the nice "modern pen" of yours, Gianni will never in his life be able to read a book. He can't write a decent letter. That is cruel punishment, way out of proportion.

2A. FULL-TIME TEACHING

Repetitions

You are quite aware that two hours a week on each subject is not enough for every student to cover the whole program.

Up to now we have had a typical upper-class solution: The poor work through the year again. To the petit bourgeois you offer coaching (for money, after school hours) so that the lessons can be reviewed. For the upper-class boys it is all taken care of, since they are repeating what they already know. Pierino has had everything explained to him at home.

The *doposcuola* is a much better solution. A boy will repeat the work in the afternoon but will not lose the year, will not spend money, and will have you with him both in guilt and in struggle.

Classless School

Let's take off the mask. As long as your school remains class oriented and chases away the poor, the only serious way to break the system is by creating a *doposcuola* that chases away the rich.

People who get upset at our solution but were never shocked at all the failing and private coaching are simply not being honest.

Pierino was not born racially different. He became different because of his environment at home, after school hours. The *doposcuola* must create a comparable environment for the rest of the children while keeping alive their own culture.

Environment

The words "full time" frighten you. You feel it is difficult enough managing the children the few hours you do now. But the truth is that you have never tried.

So far you have run your class obsessed by the school bell, and with nightmares about the curriculum to be covered by June. You haven't been able to broaden the horizons, to answer the curiosity of your young people, or to carry any argument to the very end.

The upshot is that you have done everything badly; you are always frustrated and so are the children. It is the frustration and not the hours of work that have tired you out.

2B. FULL TIME AND UNION RIGHTS

Great Fights

We happened to read a teachers' union newspaper: "No!" it said. "No, to an increase in teaching hours! There were great battles to restrict the compulsory teaching schedule, and it would be an absurdity to go back."

We felt taken aback. Strictly speaking, we can't say a word. Every worker fights to reduce his working hours and so he should.

Unusual Privileges

But your work schedule is really indecent.

A laborer works 2,150 hours a year. Your colleagues in the civil service work 1,630 hours. You, from a maximum of 738 hours (elementary teachers) to a minimum of 468 (math and foreign-language teachers).

Your explanation that you have to study and to correct papers at home is not valid. Even judges have to write out their verdicts and sentences. Then, too, you could always skip giving tests. Or if you do give them, you could correct them, together with the kids, while they are being taken.

As for your preparations and studies, we all have to study. Laborers need to study more than you do. When they take an evening course they don't ask to be paid.

School, with today's timetable, is a war against the poor. If the government can't impose longer hours of teaching, it should have nothing to do with schools.

This is a very serious conclusion. Up to now the State schools have been considered an improvement over the private. We might have to reconsider everything and put the school back in the hands of someone else. Someone with an idealistic urge to teach, and to teach to us.

2C. FULL TIME AND SUBJECT MATTER

Don Borghi*

While we were writing this letter, Don Borghi paid us a visit. He made this criticism of us: "You seem so convinced that every boy must go to school and must have a full day of it. But then the boys will turn out to be apolitical individualists, like all the other students around. Good soil for Fascism.

"As long as the teachers and the subjects they teach stay the same, the less schoolboys have, the better off they are. A workshop makes a better school.

"In order to change teachers and subject matter, we must do more than write this letter of yours. These problems must be solved at the political level."

Better Than Nothing

That's true. A Parliament that reflected the needs of all the people, and not the middle class alone, could settle both you and the school syllabus with a couple of penal laws.

But first, we have to get into Parliament. Whites will never make the laws needed by the blacks.

---

*A priest who was a friend and collaborator of Don Milani.

To get into Parliament, we have to master the language. For the time being, then, and for lack of something better, children will have to go to your kind of school.

Professional Deformity

In any case, not all teachers are as bad as Don Borghi thinks.

It may be that your deformity began while teaching at those schools. You did not favor the little gentlemen out of malice; it's just that there they were, right in front of you, for so long. Too many of them, and far too long.

You became attached to them, finally, and to their families, their world; the newspaper they read at home.

Whoever is fond of the comfortable and fortunate stays out of politics. He does not want anything to change.

The Pressure of the Poor

But now things are changing. The school population keeps growing, in spite of all your flunking.

With the masses of the poor exerting pressure, needing basic things, you cannot keep pushing a syllabus specially made for Pierino.

All the more so if you teach full time. The children of the poor will remake you and remake the syllabus.

To get to know the children of the poor and to love politics are one and the same thing. You cannot love human beings who were marked by unjust laws and not work for better laws.

3. A GOAL

An Honest Goal to Be Found

We are searching for a goal.

It must be an honest one. A great one. It must demand of a boy that he be nothing less than a human being—that would be acceptable both to believers and atheists.

I know this goal. My teacher-priest has been impressing it on me since I was eleven years old, and I thank God for it. I have saved so much time. Minute by minute. I knew why I was studying.

A Final Goal

The right goal is to give oneself to others.

In this century, how can you show your love if not through politics, the unions, and the schools? We are the sovereign people. The time for begging is gone; we must make choices— against class distinctions, against hunger, illiteracy, racism and colonial wars.

An Immediate Goal

This is the ultimate goal, which should be remembered from time to time. The immediate one, which must be remembered every minute, is to understand others and to make oneself understood.

The Italian language is not enough; it is not used very much around the world. Men need to love one another across national borders. For this we need to study many languages— living languages.

Language is made up of words from every subject matter. So we must touch all subjects, at least lightly, in order to enrich our vocabulary. We must become amateurs in everything and specialists only in the ability to speak.

Sovereigns

It is the language alone that makes men equal. That man is an equal who can express himself and can understand the words of others. Rich or poor, it makes no difference. But he must speak.

When we all have the power to speak, the social climbers can go on with their own studies. Let them go to the university, grab all the diplomas, make piles of money, and fill all the specialists' jobs.

As long as they don't ask for a larger share of power, as they have up to now.

Wither Away

Poor Pierino, I almost feel sorry for you. You have paid dearly for your privileges. You are marked forever by your specialization, by your books, and by contact with people all just like you. Why don't you quit?

Leave the university, your obligations, your political parties. Start teaching right away. Start teaching the language and nothing else.

Break a path for the poor, forgetting about yourself. Stop reading. Wither away. It is the final mission of your class.

PART II

In the *Magistrale*
You Also Flunk, But . . .

ENGLAND

The Real Test

When I passed my exams and left the intermediate school I went to England. I was fifteen. At first I worked with a farmer in Canterbury; later on, with a wine merchant in London.

In our school the experience of going abroad takes the place of your exams. But it is an exam and a school wrapped up in one. We test our culture by sifting it through life.

Our final exam is far more difficult than the one you give, but at least while taking it we don't lose time on dead things.

Suez

My exam went well. I came home alive and even brought back some cash. Best of all, I came back bursting with new experiences which I had understood and which I was able to retell.

The only member of the family who had ever gone abroad before was my Uncle Renato. He went to war, in Ethiopia.

You will never get me to go abroad like him, to start killing farmers. I went and lived in a farmer's house. There was a boy my age. A younger daughter, too. They have a barn, they grow potatoes, they toil away like us. Why should I kill them!

Against a Wall

When I returned to Italy I had forgotten that I was timid.

To explain oneself at the borders of countries, to argue with the boss and with monarchists, to defend oneself from racists and faggots, to save money, make decisions, eat strange food, wait for letters, and swallow nostalgia: I felt I had tried and conquered everything.

But one thing I had not lived through was the *magistrale*. Now I've tried it. It has been like banging my head against a wall.

Either You or Us

And yet, my schoolmates have broken through all over. Some of them are full-time union officials, and doing very well. Others are in various factories in Florence and nobody can intimidate them. They work in the unions, in politics, and in the local administrations.

Even the two who went to the technical school have done well. They get promoted, like the Pierinos.

Our own culture bears up well wherever there is real life. In the *magistrale* it is useless.

SUICIDAL SELECTION

Forgetful

In the first part of this letter we tried to show what great damage is done to the discarded children. [But] the worst damage of all is done to the select.

The child who gets promoted stays with the same class. He is more of a fixture than his teachers. He should be able to make friends with his schoolmates and to take an interest in how they turn out.

But there are too many of them. Within eight years forty schoolmates have been sliced away from him or have burned up like dry branches. At the end of the intermediate school another five have dropped out—even though they were promoted—and so that makes forty-five. Pierino never hears a thing about them or their problems.

Snooty

In the second grade Pierino was one boy among many. By the fifth, he belongs to a more restricted group. Forty children out of the hundred he meets along the way have already become his "inferiors."

After graduating from the intermediate school his "inferiors" have multiplied to ninety out of a hundred. After the upper-school diploma they are ninety-six. After his college degree, ninety-nine.

Every year he has seen higher marks put on his report card than on those of his disappearing schoolmates. The teachers who give those marks have engraved on his soul the impression that the other ninety-nine belong to an inferior culture.

At this stage, it would be a miracle if his soul did not become crippled.

The Poor Have a Reward

His soul indeed is sick, because his teachers have lied to him. The culture of those other ninety-nine is not inferior; it is different.

True culture, which no man has yet possessed, would be made up of two elements: belonging to the masses and mastery of the language.

A school that is as selective as the kind we have described destroys culture. It deprives the poor of the means of expressing themselves. It deprives the rich of the knowledge of things as they are.

Unlucky Gianni, who can't express himself. Lucky Gianni, because he belongs to the whole world: brother to the whole of Africa, Asia, and Latin America. Expert in the needs of most of humanity.

Lucky Pierino, because he can speak. Unlucky, because he speaks too much. He, who has nothing important to say. He, who repeats only things read in books written by others just like him. He, who is locked up in a refined little circle—cut off from history and geography.

The selective school is a sin against God and against men. But God has defended his poor. You want them to be mute, and so God has made you blind.

Potential Fascists

Most of my schoolmates from Florence never read a newspaper. Those who do, read the paper of the Establishment. I asked one of them once if he knew who financed it. "Nobody. It's independent."

They don't care to know anything about politics. One of them did not even know the meaning of the word "union."

What they have heard about strikes is that they are a device for ruining production. They don't question the truth of this.

Three of them are out-and-out Fascists.

Twenty-eight apolitical plus three Fascists equals thirty-one Fascists.

Even Blinder

There are students and intellectuals of a somewhat different type: They read everything and are militant left-wingers. Nevertheless, they can seem even blinder.

The most leftist teacher I have heard was giving a talk to a meeting of teachers and parents. When it came to the *doposcuola*, he burst out with: "You don't seem to realize that I teach a good eighteen hours a week!"

The room was crowded with workers who get up at four in the morning to catch the 5:39 train and with farmers who work eighteen hours every day, all summer. Nobody spoke or smiled. Fifty blank pairs of eyes were fixed on him in silence.

THE GOAL

Bitter Fruit

The fruit of a selective system is a bitter fruit that will never ripen. I soon realized that most of my schoolmates were going to the *magistrale* either by chance or because their parents had made the choice.

When I appeared at the front door of your school I was carrying a new briefcase. It was a present from my young pupils. At the age of fifteen I had already earned my first compensation as a teacher.

I never told this either to you or to my schoolmates. That may have been a mistake on my part, but your school is not a place for speaking out. When somebody knows what he wants, and wants to do something worthwhile, he is taken for an idiot.

Stingy

None of my schoolmates spoke of teaching. I know it must be discouraging for you to try to explain what a teacher is to the kind of boys you have in your classes. Still—is it the boys who have ruined you, or is it you who have ruined them?

Because of the increasing possibility to apply to the university after the *magistrale* instead of going into teaching, the training in the *magistrale* is becoming ever more generalized and vague.

To produce good teachers we need a self-contained school, one that is not a stepping-stone to other fields. The boy who wants to work in a bank should feel like an outsider in such a school. The boy from the farms who has chosen to become a teacher should feel at home.

These schools educate citizens specialized in serving others. They have to be reliable.

The teaching diploma should be hard to get. We don't want to be cut down later on. We should be treated the same as chemists, doctors, and engineers.

An Eye on the Goal

You do not fail a taxi driver if he doesn't know math, or a doctor who doesn't know his poets.

Once you said to me in these precise words, "You see, you don't know enough Latin. Why don't you go to a technical school?"

Are you sure that Latin is indispensable to the making of a good teacher? Have you given it any thought? All you do is keep your eye on the system as it is; but you never really evaluate it.

The Individual

If you had taken a real interest in me, enough to ask yourself where I came from, who I was, where I was heading, then your Latin would have gone out of focus.

But you might have found something else to object to in me. It frightens you to see a fifteen-year-old boy who knows what he wants. You sense the influence of his teacher.

Woe unto him who toys with the Individual! The Free Development of the Personality is your highest creed. The needs of society are no concern of yours at all.

I am a boy under the influence of my teacher and I am proud of it. He, too, is proud of it. What, if not this, is the essence of a school?

School is the one difference between men and animals. The teacher gives to a boy everything the teacher himself believes, loves, and hopes for. The boy, growing up, will add something of his own, and this is the way humanity moves forward.

Animals don't go to school. In the Free Development of their Personality, swallows have built their nests in exactly the same way for millennia.

The Seminary

I have been told that even in the seminary there are boys torturing themselves to find their vocation. If they had been told in elementary school that we all have the same vocation—to do good wherever we are—then they would not have to lose the best years of their lives worrying about themselves.

School of Social Service

We could allow a bit more time for final choices by having two different types of schools.

One, for fourteen to eighteen year olds, could be called the "School of Social Service." It would be for anybody who has already decided to give his life to others. The same schooling could serve for priests, elementary school teachers, union workers, and men in politics. One year might be added for specialization.

We could call all the other schools "Schools of Ego Service," and they could continue to be the schools that we have now, without changing them.

High Aims

The School of Social Service could try to aim high and find pleasure in it. No grades, no grade book, no games, no holidays, no weakness about marriage or a career. All the students would be guided toward total dedication.

Along the way some might settle a bit lower. They might find girls and adjust themselves to loving a more limited family.

They will be much better off for having spent their best years preparing to serve an immense family—the family of man.

They will make better fathers and mothers, full of ideals, ready to raise a child who in turn will go back to that same school.

Your School of Ego Service wants to prepare everyone for marriage. It is not much of a success even for those who marry. And when someone stays single, he becomes a bitter spinster-man.

THE CULTURE NEEDED BY ALL

Exodus

In the mountains we can't survive. In the fields there are too many of us. All the economists agree on that point.

And what if they didn't agree? Try and put yourself in my parents' shoes. You would not allow your son to be shunted aside. Therefore, you ought to welcome us in your midst—and not as a second-class citizens good only for unskilled work.

Every People has its own culture, and no people has less than the others. Our culture is a gift that we bring to you. A vital breath of air to relieve the dryness of your books written by men who have done nothing but read books.

All Alone Like Dogs

You know even less about men than we do. The lift serves as a good machine for ignoring the people in your building; the car, for ignoring people who travel in buses; the telephone, for avoiding seeing people's faces or entering their homes.

I don't know about you, but your students who know Cicero—how many families of living men do they know intimately? How many of their kitchens have they visited? How many of their sick have they sat with through the night? How many of their dead have they borne on their shoulders? How many can they trust when they are in distress?

If it hadn't been for the flood in Florence* they wouldn't know how many people there are in the family that lives on the ground floor.

---

*The great flood of 1966.

I was in a class for a year with these young people, but I have no idea what their families are like. And yet they never stop jabbering. Often they raise their voices to a pitch so high no one can possibly understand them. In any case, each one only wants to listen to himself.

Human Culture

A thousand motors roar under your windows every day. You have no idea to whom they belong or where they are going.

But I can read the sounds of my valley for miles around. The sound of the motor in the distance is Nevio going to the station, a little late. If you like, I can tell you everything about hundreds of people, dozens of families and their relatives and personal ties.

Whenever you speak to a worker you manage to get it all wrong: your choice of words, your tone, your jokes. I can tell what a mountaineer is thinking even when he keeps silent, and I know what's on his mind even when he talks about something else.

This is the sort of culture your poets should have given you. It is the culture of nine-tenths of the earth, but no one has yet managed to put it down in words or pictures or films.

Be a bit humble, at least. Your culture has gaps as wide as ours. Perhaps even wider. Certainly more damaging to a teacher in the elementary schools.

THE CULTURE THAT YOU DEMAND OF *US*

Philosophy

Any philosopher studied out of a handbook becomes a bore. There are too many philosophers and they say too many things.

My philosophy teacher never took a stand for or against any of them. I could not work out whether he liked them all or simply didn't care.

If I have to choose between two teachers, one a nut on the subject and the other totally indifferent, I'll take the nut—the one who has a theory of his own, or prefers a particular philosopher. He is certain to talk only about that philosopher and to attack all the others, but he would make us read the original writings of that philosopher during all of our three years of school. We would come out knowing that philosophy can fill an entire life.

Pedagogy

The way pedagogy is taught today, I would skip it altogether—although I'm not quite sure. Perhaps if we go deeper into it, we could decide whether or not it has something to say. We might discover that it says one thing and one thing only. That each boy is different, each historical moment is different, and so is every moment different for each boy, each country, each environment, and each family.

Half a page from the textbook is all that is needed to explain this; the rest we can tear up and throw away.

At the school of Barbiana not a day went by without its pedagogical problem. But we never called it by that name. For us, it always had the name of a particular boy. Case after case, time after time.

I don't think there is a treatise written by any professor that can tell us anything about Gianni that we don't already know.

History

There are several different history surveys. They are narrow-minded, one-sided little tales passed down to the peasants by the conqueror. Italy right in the center of the world. The losers always bad, the winners all-good. There is talk only of kings, generals, and stupid wars among nations. The sufferings and struggles of the workers are either ignored or stuck into a corner.

Woe unto the man disliked by generals and armament makers! In the best, most "modern" book, Gandhi is disposed of in nine lines. Without a word on his thoughts, and even less on his methods.

Civics

Civics is another subject that I know something about, but it does not come up in your schools.

Some teachers say, as an excuse, that it is taught by implication through other subjects. If this were true, it would be too good to believe. If that really is such a great way to teach something, then why don't they use it for all subjects, building a sound structure in which all the elements are blended together and yet can be extracted separately at any time?

Admit that in truth you have hardly any knowledge of civics. You have only a vague notion of what a mayor really is. You have never had dinner in the home of a worker. You don't know the terms of the pending issue on public transport. You only know that the traffic jams are upsetting your private life.

You have never studied these problems, because they scare you. As it also scares you to plunge into the deeper meanings of geography. Your textbook covers all the world but never mentions hunger, monopolies, political systems, or racism.

Comments

One subject is totally missing from your syllabuses: the art of writing.

It is enough simply to see some of the comments you write at the top of your students' compositions. I have a choice collection of them, right here. They are all nothing more than assertions—never a means for improving the work.

"Childish. Infantile. Shows immaturity. Poor. Trivial." What use can a boy make of this sort of thing! Perhaps he should send his grandfather to school; he's more mature.

Other comments: "Meager contents. Poor conception. Pale ideas. No real participation in what you wrote." The theme must have been wrong, then. It ought not to have been assigned.

Or: "Try to improve your form. Incorrect form. Cramped. Unclear. Not well constructed. Poor usage. Try to write more simply. Sentence structure all wrong. Your way of expressing yourself is not always felicitous. You must have better control of your means of expression." You are the one who should have taught all that. But you don't even believe that writing can be taught; you don't believe there are any objective rules for the art of writing; you are still embalmed in your nineteenth-century individualism.

Then we also meet the creature touched by the hands of gods: "Spontaneous. Rich flow of ideas. Fitting use of your ideas, in harmony with a striking personality." Having gone that far, why not just add: "Blessed be the mother who gave you birth"?

The Genius

You returned one of my compositions with a very low grade and this comment: "Writers are born, not made." Meanwhile you receive a salary as a teacher of Italian.

The theory of the genius is a bourgeois invention. It was born from a compound of racism and laziness.

It is also useful in politics. Rather than having to steer through the complex of existing parties, you find it easier to get hold of a de Gaulle, call him a genius, and say that he is France.

This is the way you operate in your Italian class. Pierino has the gift. I do not. So let's all relax about it.

It doesn't matter whether or nor Pierino reflects on his writing. He will write more of those books that already surround him. Five hundred pages that could be reduced to fifty without losing a single idea.

I can learn resignation and go back to the woods.

As for you, you can go on lounging behind your desk and making little marks in your grade book.

School of Art

The craft of writing is to be taught like any other craft.

But at Barbiana we had to argue this question among ourselves. One faction wanted to describe the way we go about writing. Others said, "Art is a serious matter, even if it uses simple techniques. The readers will laugh at us."

The poor will not laugh at us. The rich can go on laughing all they want and we shall laugh at them, not able to write either a book or a newspaper with the skill of the poor.

Finally we agreed to write down everything for readers who will love us.

A Humble Technique

This is the way we do it:

To start with, each of us keeps a notebook in his pocket. Every time an idea comes up, we make a note of it. Each idea on a separate sheet, on one side of the page.

Then one day we gather together all the sheets of paper and spread them on a big table. We look through them one by one, to get rid of duplications. Next, we make separate piles of the sheets that are related, and these will make up the chapters. Every chapter is subdivided into small piles, and they will become paragraphs.

At this point we try to give a title to each paragraph. If we can't it means either that the paragraph has no content or that many things are squeezed into it. Some paragraphs disappear. Some are broken up.

While we name the paragraphs we discuss their logical order, until an outline is born. With the outline set, we reorganize all the piles to follow its pattern.

We take the first pile, spread the sheets on the table, and we find the sequence for them. And so we begin to put down a first draft of the text.

We duplicate that part so that we each can have a copy in front of us. Then scissors, paste, and colored pencils. We shuffle it all again. New sheets are added. We duplicate again.

A race begins now for all of us to find any word that can be crossed out, any excess adjectives, repetitions, lies, difficult words, over-long sentences, and any two concepts that are forced into one sentence.

We call in one outsider after another. We prefer it if they have not had too much schooling. We ask them to read aloud. And we watch to see if they have understood what we meant to say.

We accept their suggestions if they clarify the text. We reject any suggestions made in the name of caution.

Having done all this hard work and having followed these rules that anyone can use, we often come across an intellectual idiot who announces, "This letter has a remarkably personal style."

Laziness

Why don't you admit that you don't know what the art of writing is? It is an art that is the very opposite of laziness.

And don't say that you lack the time for it. It would be enough to have one long paper written throughout the year, but written by all the students together.

CRIMINAL TRIAL

You work 210 days a year, of which thirty are lost in giving exams and over thirty more on tests. That leaves only 150 days of school in a year. Half of these school days are lost in oral examinations, which means that there are seventy-five days of teaching against 135 of passing judgment.

Without changing your working contract in the least, you could triple the hours of schooling you give.

Tests in the Classroom

While giving a test you used to walk up and down between the rows of desks and see me in trouble and making mistakes, but you never said a word.

I have the same situation at home. No one to run to for help for miles around. No books. No telephone.

Now here I am in "school." I came from far away to be taught. Here I don't have to deal with my mother, who promised to be quiet and then interrupted me a hundred times.

My sister's little boy is not here to ask me for help with his homework. Here I have silence and good light and a desk all to myself.

And over there, a few steps away, you stand. You know all of these things. You are paid to help me.

Instead, you waste your time keeping me under guard as if I were a thief.

Laziness and Terror

You yourself told me that oral examinations are not really school. "When my class is given the first hour you can take a later train, since I spend the first half-hour at oral exams."

During those exams the whole class sinks either into laziness or terror. Even the boy being questioned wastes his time. He keeps taking cover, avoids what he understands least, keeps stressing the things he knows well.

To make you happy we need know only how to sell our goods. And how never to keep quiet. And how to fill empty spaces with empty words.

Personal Opinions

It's even better to air some "personal opinions." You hold these personal opinions in high regard: "In my opinion, Petrarch . . ." Perhaps this boy has read two of his poems, perhaps none.

I have heard that in certain American schools whenever the teacher says anything, half the students raise their hands and say, "I agree!" The other half says, "I don't." Then they change sides, continuing to chew gum all the while with great energy.

A student who gives personal opinions on things beyond his reach is an imbecile. He should not be praised for it. One goes to school to listen to the teachers.

It can happen on rare occasions that something of our own might be useful to the class or to the teacher. Not just an opinion or something quoted out of a book. Some definite thing seen with our own eyes, at home, in the streets, or in the woods.

A Clever Question

You never asked me questions about such things. On my own, I would never speak out about them. But your young gentlemen could go on asking, with angelic faces, about all sorts of things they already knew. And you would keep encouraging them: "What a clever question!"

A comedy useless to everyone concerned. Harmful to those bootlickers. Cruel to me, who was unable to be good at that game.

Blackmail

Meanwhile the minutes were passing and my mouth would not open. I was sunk in rage and despair. Those pathetic children couldn't make me out.

No one disliked me. Not even you: "I'm not going to eat you up." You sounded so encouraging. You wanted to do your duty by me.

And meanwhile you were destroying every single ideal I had, with the blackmail power of that diploma you have in your hands.

Art

If I had had some time to calm down during those oral examinations (as I now have with my friends while we write these things) I could have convinced you. I'm sure of it. You are not a beast, after all.

At the moment, though, only filthy words and insults kept coming to my mind. Those words that we try hard to hold back while we transform them into arguments.

Slowly the truth will emerge from beneath the hatred. The work of art is born: a hand held out to your enemy so that he may change.

INFECTION

After a month at your school I, too, was infected.

During the oral exams my heart would stop beating. I found that I was wishing on others what I did not want done to myself.

I stopped listening to the lessons. I would think only about the oral exams coming up in the next hour.

The best and most exciting subjects—wrapped up and lifeless. As if they had no relationship to the larger world outside. As if they could be confined only to those inches between the blackboard and the teacher's desk.

A Worm

At home, I didn't even notice when my mother fell ill. Nor did I have any interest in my neighbors. I never read a newspaper. I couldn't sleep at night.

My mother cried. My father grumbled through his teeth: "You'd be better off out in the woods."

I was reduced to studying like a worm.

Until then, I had always had time to approach something as I would if I were teaching it to my pupils. If something seemed important, I would drop the textbook and go deeper into other books to understand it.

After your treatment, I found even the textbook too much. I saw myself underlining the crucial points. Later, my schoolmates suggested even skinnier books for cramming, invented strictly for satisfying your little heads.

Doubts

I reached the point of thinking you were right, and that your culture was the true one. Perhaps we, in our solitude up there, were still dreaming with simplicity you had left behind centuries ago.

Perhaps our dream of a language that everyone could read, made of plain words, was nothing but a fantasy ahead of its time.

By a hair I missed becoming one of you. Like those children of the poor who change their race when they go up to the university.

The Outrider

I did not quite have the time, though, to become as corrupt as you would have liked. In June you gave me a 5 in Italian and a 4 in Latin (out of a possible 10).

I took the old path through the woods once more and returned to Barbiana. Day after day, from dawn till dark, like a child again.

But I did not pick up the full schedule of the school. Because of the two exams I had to repeat, my mentor relieved me from having to teach the younger pupils and from reading the newspaper. I was allowed to study in a room all by myself in order to have silence and the books I did not have at home.

I used to return from the dead only for the reading of the mail.

Annibal Caro

When all the letters are read, I shut myself up again with my Aenead.*

I read an episode that you like.

Two toughs are disemboweling people while they sleep. List of: people disemboweled, the stolen goods, the names of the men who have given a belt as a gift and the weight of that belt. The whole thing in a stillborn language.

The Aenead was not part of the curriculum. You chose it. I will never forgive you that.

My friends, however, do forgive me. They know that my goal is to be a teacher. But I am just as cut off from things as you are.

———

*Annibal Caro: 16th-century translator of *The Aenead*.

DISINFECTION

Superficial

In September you gave me 4s on both tests. You can't even carry out your pharmacist's trade very well. Your little scales are not working. How could I know less than I did in June?

You flipped a switch. You switched off a boy. But actually, without knowing it, you turned on my light. You opened my eyes to you and your culture.

First of all I have found the most accurate insult for defining you: you are simply superficial. You are a society of mutual flatterers that survives because there are so few of you.

Revenge

My father and my brother go off to the woods for me. I cannot repeat that class again and I do not intend to carry wood on my back, letting the world go on the way it is. That would give you too much satisfaction.

So I was back in Barbiana, and in June I went to take the exam once more.

You flunked me again, as if you were spitting on the ground. But I am not going to give up. I will be a teacher and I'll make a better teacher than you.

Second Revenge

My other revenge is this letter. We all worked on it together.

Even Gianni did some work. His father is in the hospital. If only Gianni had been as manly last year as he is now. But now it is too late for schooling. They need his apprentice's pay at home. When he heard about this letter, though, he promised to come and help us on Sundays.

He finally came. He read it. He pointed out some words or phrases that were too difficult. He reminded us of some tasty bits of viciousness. He authorized us to make fun of him. He is practically the chief author.

But don't let yourself take comfort from this. You still have to carry him around in your soul. He can't yet express himself.

Waiting for an Answer

Now we are here awaiting an answer. There must be someone in some *magistrale* who will write to us:

"Dear boys,

"Not all teachers are like that lady of yours. Don't become racists yourselves.

"Although I can't agree with everything you say, I know that our school isn't good enough. Only a perfect school can afford to refuse new people and new cultures. And there is no perfect school. Neither yours nor ours.

"However, if any of you who want to be teachers will come and take your examinations here, I have a group of colleagues ready to shut their eyes for your sake.

"In pedagogy, we shall ask you only about Gianni. In literature, we shall ask how you wrote this beautiful letter. In Latin, some old words your grandfather still uses. In geography, the customs of English farmers. In history, the reasons why mountain people come down to the plains. In science, you can tell us about *sormenti** and give us the correct name of the tree that bears cherries."

We are waiting for this letter. We know it will come.

---

*Twig; vine-shoot.

Postscript: Immortality

I have been to Italy many times, although never to the area that gave birth to this book. Since beginning work on this project, I have dreamed of entering that tiny cemetery to pay tribute to the dead priest and his students. The cemetery, the town, and the region are surrounded by a very different Italy from the one Don Lorenzo knew. The power of the church has waned, agriculture has taken a backseat to industry and commerce, family size has shrunk, consumption has burgeoned, the openness to other countries and cultures which Father Milani valued so highly has expanded exponentially, radical politics has given way to the crass Berlusconi years. Yet poverty and injustice still exist, now more concentrated in the faces of the people of color who have flocked to Italy and its European neighbors in search of a fate better than the one that awaited them at home.

There is always work for the Father Milanis, the teachers who believe it is their job to prepare students to make a more equitable world. The only form of immortality of which we can be sure is the kind being enacted by those Schoolboys, 40 years removed from the presbytery at Barbiana, who are working as public health nurses in Third World countries, as union organizers closer to home, as community activists creating change from the bottom up. In the words of Bill Ayers, "Teachers might not change the world in dramatic fashion, but we certainly change the people who will change the world."

Letter of Don Lorenzo Milani to the Military Chaplains of Tuscany Who Signed the Communiqué of 11 February 1965

Within less than a month Milani and his pupils composed a reply to the chaplains' communiqué that Milani signed, had printed, and sent round to all the local clergy. He also sent it to a number of newspapers and magazines. It appeared in its entirety in La Rinascita, *a magazine published in Rome by the Communist Party of Italy.*

For some time now I have wanted to have one of you speak to my youngsters about your life. It is a life that the children and I do not understand.

Still, we would have wanted to make an effort to understand, and especially to ask you how you have coped with some of the practical problems of military life. But I did not act soon enough to organize this meeting between you and my school.

My preference would have been to talk of these things privately, but now that you have taken up the issue publicly, and in a newspaper, I have no choice but to address these questions to you publicly.

First: why have you insulted citizens whom we and many other people admire? No one, as far as I am aware, had raised a voice against you. Possibly the simple consistency of their heroic Christian example aggravates some internal insecurity within yourselves.

Second: why have you used, in an offhand and undefined way, words that are oversized for you?

This English translation of Father Milani's letter first appeared in *A Just War No Longer Exists*, ed. and trans. James T. Burtchaell (Notre Dame, IN: University of Notre Dame Press, 1988). Reprinted with the permission of the University of Notre Dame Press.

Before you reply, keep in mind that public opinion today is more mature than it used to be, and will not be satisfied either by silence on your part, or by a vague retort that ignores our specific questions. Sentimental slogans or vulgar insults directed at conscientious objectors or at me are not arguments. If you have arguments I will be happy to acknowledge them, and to correct myself if in the impulse of my writing I should have expressed myself unfairly.

I shall not discuss here the idea of Fatherland as such. It involves a distinction with which I do not agree. If you persist in claiming the right to divide the world into Italians and foreigners, then I must say to you that, in your view of things, I have no Fatherland. I would then want the right to divide the world into disinherited and oppressed on one side, and privileged and oppressors on the other. One group is my Fatherland; to me, the others are foreigners. And if, without being disciplined by the church, you have the right to teach that it can be a moral thing—even heroic—for Italians and foreigners to tear each other to pieces, I claim the right to say that then the poor can and should take up arms against the rich.

At least in the choice of weapons we enjoy the advantage. The arms that you condone are horrible devices of war to kill, to mutilate, to destroy, to make widows and orphans. The only weapons I condone are noble and bloodless: the strike and the ballot.

We have, then, very different ideas. I can respect yours if you manage to justify them in light of the Gospel or the Constitution. But you too must respect the ideas of others. Especially if they are people who pay for their ideas in person.

You will surely agree that the word "Fatherland" is often put to improper use. Frequently it serves simply as a pretext to dispense oneself from reflection, or from the study of history, or from making choices, on occasion, between the Fatherland and even nobler values.

In this letter I do not wish to appeal to the Gospel. It is all too easy to demonstrate that Jesus was opposed to violence and that he did not accept even legitimate self-defense, per se. I shall refer instead to the Constitution:

> Article 11: "Italy condemns war as an instrument of aggression against the liberties of other peoples . . ."[1]
> Article 52: "Defense of the Fatherland is a sacred duty of the citizen."

Let us use this standard to take the measure of the wars to which the Italian people have been summoned throughout the one century of our history.

If we should find that the history of our army is implicated in offenses against the Fatherlands of others, you then ought to clarify for us whether in those cases the soldiers should have obeyed, or should have raised the objections presented by their consciences. And then you ought to explain who *defended* the Fatherland and its honor more: those who objected or those who by their obedience made our Fatherland odious in the eyes of the entire civilized world? Spare us the high-flown or evasive speeches. Get down to the facts. Tell us just what you have taught the soldiers. Obedience at all costs? What if the orders were for the bombardment of civilians, a reprisal mission against a defenseless village, the summary execution of partisans, the use of atomic or bacteriological or chemical weapons, torture, the execution of hostages, drum-head trial of mere suspects, decimation (selecting every tenth soldier of the Fatherland and then shooting him to strike fear into the other soldiers of the Fatherland), a war of obvious aggression, an order from an officer in revolt against the sovereign people, or the repression of public demonstration. These actions and many others of the sort are the daily bread of every war. When they took place in front of your eyes either you lied or you kept silent. Or do you wish us to believe that you have been insisting on the truth time after time, eye-to-eye with your "superiors," in defiance of prison or death? If you still have your lives and your promotions, it must be a sign that you have raised no objections at all. In any case you have demonstrated conclusively by your communiqué that you have not the slightest notion of the concept of conscientious objection.

You cannot avoid making a judgment on the events of yesteryear if you wish to be—as you should be—the moral mentors of our soldiers. To begin with, the Fatherland—we, that is—are paying you or have paid you for that very purpose. And if we maintain a very expensive army (one trillion lire a year), it is only so that it can defend both the Fatherland and the high values which that concept comprises: sovereignty of the people, freedom, justice. And that is all the more reason why, with history books in hand, you should have educated our soldiers for objection rather than for obedience

Throughout these one hundred years of history they have known all too little objection. To their shame and that of the world, they have known all too much obedience.

Let us page through history together. In each instance you must tell us which side represented the Fatherland; which direction we should have fired in; when it was right to obey; and when, to object.

1860. An army of Neapolitans, consumed by their patriotic zeal, tried to drive into the sea a handful of brigands which was attacking their Fatherland. Among those brigands there were various Neapolitan officers who were deserters from their Fatherland. It was, to be precise, the brigands who won. Today every one of them has a statue in some Italian piazza commemorating him as a hero of the Fatherland.[2]

One hundred years later history repeats itself. Europe is at our gates. The Constitution hastens to greet her: "Italy agrees to the necessary limitations of sovereignty. . . ."[3] Our children will laugh at your concept of Fatherland, just as we all now laugh at the Fatherland of the Bourbons. And our grandchildren will laugh at that of Europe. The uniforms of the soldiers and of the military chaplains will be on display only in museums.

The war following 1866 was another war of aggression. In fact, we made an alliance with the most truculent, war-mongering nation in the world to collaborate in a joint attack on Austria.[4]

The wars of 1867–1870 against the Romans were surely wars of aggression. The Romans were not very fond of their civil Fatherland, and they did little to defend it. But neither were they fond of their new Fatherland that was invading them, nor did they rise up to hasten its victory. As Gregorovius explained it in his diary: "The uprising scheduled for today has been cancelled due to rain."[5]

In 1898 the "Gallant" King bestowed the Grand Military Cross on General Bava-Beccaris for his services in a war it is good for us to remember. The enemy was a crowd of beggars who were waiting for some soup outside a convent in Milan. The General hit them with a bombardment of cannons and mortars simply because the rich (yesterday just like today) demanded the privilege of not paying taxes. They wanted to raise the tax on cornmeal, to shift more burden onto the poor, and off their own shoulders. They got what they wanted. There were eighty dead, and countless wounded. Among the soldiers there was not a single man wounded, nor a single man who objected. When their army service was over they went home to eat polenta. Not much of it, though, for it had become more expensive.[6]

Then their officers had them shouting for "Savoy!" when they sent them twice (1896 and 1935) to invade a distant and peaceful people who were in no way threatening the borders of our Fatherland. These were the only black people who had not previously been wasted by the plague of European colonialism.[7]

When whites and blacks are fighting, are you with the whites? Is it not enough to impose on us the Italian Fatherland? Do you also want to impose the White Race Fatherland? Are you the kind of priests who read *La Nazione*? Read it carefully, for it is a newspaper that considers the life of one white worth more than the lives of one hundred blacks. You have seen the coverage it gave to the killing of sixty whites in the Congo, but it forgot to describe the appalling slaughter of blacks and to identify the whites who are directing it all from Europe.

The same for the war in Libya.[8]

Then we come to 1914. Italy attacks Austria of which, this time, it had been an ally.

Was Battisti a patriot or a deserter?[9] It is a minor detail, but one you should clear up if you want to talk about Fatherland. Did you tell our boys that that was a war we could have avoided? That Giolitti knew for certain that he could obtain gratis what he ended up obtaining with 600,000 deaths? That the overwhelming majority of the Chamber of Deputies was ready to support him (450 out of 508)?[10] Was it then the Fatherland that did the calling to arms? And if it did issue the call, was it not perhaps to a "useless carnage"? (The expression comes, not from a cowardly conscientious objector, but from a canonized Pope.)[11]

In 1922 the Fatherland needed to be defended against attack. But the army did not defend it. It stood in wait for the orders that never came.[12] If their priests had educated them to be guided by *conscience* instead of by "blind, swift, and absolute" *obedience*, how many sorrows might have been spared the Fatherland and the world (50,000,000 dead).[13] As it turned out, the Fatherland fell into the power of a handful of criminals who violated every law, human and divine, and, with their mouths full of the word "Fatherland," brought the country to catastrophe. In those tragic years, the priests who had nothing but the sacred word "Fatherland" in their minds and mouths, who never desired to deepen the sense and resonance of that expression, who spoke as you now speak-those priests did a pathetic injury to the Fatherland (and, be it said in passing, they also dishonored the church).

In 1936, 50,000 Italian troops found themselves embarked on a new and infamous aggression. They had all filled out the statutory "volunteer's card" in order to join in an attack on the hapless Spanish people.[14]

They ran to the aid of a general who was a traitor to his Fatherland, a rebel against his lawful government and his sovereign people.[15] With the help of Italy, and at the cost of a million and a half lives, he succeeded in obtaining what the rich wanted: wage controls without price controls, abolition of strikes, of unions, of political parties, of every civil and religious liberty. Still today, in defiance of the rest of the world, that revolting general imprisons, tortures, kills (even garrots) whoever is guilty of having defended the Fatherland then or of trying to do so now. Without the obedience of the Italian "volunteers" this would never have happened.

If, in those sad times, there had not been Italians on the other side as well, none of us could look a Spaniard in the eye today.[16] Those Italians were, to be precise, rebels and exiles from their own Fatherland. They were people who had objected. Have you said to your soldiers where their duty would lie if they should have a general like Franco? Have you explained that officers who disobey their sovereign, the people, must not be obeyed?

Then, from 1939 onwards there was a landslide: the Italian soldiers attacked six other Fatherlands, one after the other, which had certainly not attacked their own: Albania, France, Greece, Egypt, Yugoslavia, Russia.[17] It was an Italian war that had two fronts: one against the democratic system; the other, against the socialist. They were and still are the two noblest political systems mankind has yet been given. One represents the highest attempt of humankind to give, already on this earth, liberty and human dignity to the poor. The other represents the highest attempt of humankind to give, already on this earth, justice and equality to the poor.

Don't go to the effort of answering by accusing these systems of their respective faults and mistakes. We know that these are human things. Tell us instead what we were offering in their place: without a doubt the worst political system that unscrupulous oppressors have ever been able to dream up. It was a rejection of every moral value, and every liberty except for the rich and for the perverse. A rejection of every justice and of all religion. Propaganda of hate and extermination of innocents. One result, among others, was the extermination of the Jews, the Fatherland of the Lord, dispersed and suffering across the world.

What befell the Fatherland through all that? And what could be the meaning of Fatherlands at war now, after that last war when it was really ideologies, and not Fatherlands, that stood in opposition?

At last, during this hundred years of Italian history there was also one "just" war . . . if such a thing exists. It was the only war in which other Fatherlands were the aggressors and ours was on the defensive: the war of resistance by the partisans. On one side were civilians; on the other, military. On one side they were soldiers who had obeyed; on the other, soldiers who had objected. Which of the two forces, in your judgment, were the rebels and which were the regulars? It is a notion that needs to be clear if you are going to talk about Fatherland. In the Congo, for instance, who are the rebels?

Eventually, thank God, our Fatherland lost the unjust war which it had unleashed. The Fatherlands attacked by our Fatherland succeeded in driving back our troops.

Certainly we owe those troops our respect. They were hapless farmers or workers who were turned into aggressors by military obedience. The same military obedience that you chaplains glorify without a single *distinguo* to relate it to St. Peter's question: "Is it God or men that we ought to obey?"[18] n yet you heap injury on a few courageous men who have ended up in prison for doing what St. Peter did.

In many civilized countries (more civilized, in this regard, than our own) the law respects them by allowing them to serve the Fatherland in another way. They are asking to make greater sacrifices for the Fatherland, not lesser ones. They are not to blame if in Italy similar men have no choice but to serve their Fatherland idly in prison.

There is, as a matter of fact, a law in Italy which does recognize conscientious objection. It is the very Concordat which you were intending to commemorate.[19] Its third article sanctions the outright conscientious objection of bishops and priests.

As for other objectors, the church has yet made no pronouncement either for them or against them. The human sentence imposed on them is simply that they have disobeyed the law of men, not that they are cowards. Who has authorized you to add insult to that injury? When you call them cowards, do you ever recall anyone saying that cowardice is the exception and heroism the rule?

Hold back your insults. Perhaps tomorrow you will find that these men are prophets. Admittedly, the place of prophets is in prison, but it is not very becoming to take sides with whoever put them there.

If you tell us that you have chosen the vocation of chaplains in order to help the wounded and the dying, that is an idea we can respect. Gandhi as a young man did the same. When he was older he harshly disavowed that error of his youth. Have you read his life?

But if you tell us that the refusal to defend oneself and' one's own according to the example and the commandment of our Lord is "alien to the Christian commandment of love," then you are not aware of what Spirit you belong to! What kind of language are you using? How can we listen to you if you use words without measuring their meaning? If you do not wish to honor the suffering of the objectors, have the goodness at least to be still!

Our hopes are the contrary of what you hope for. Our hope is that finally there be an end to all discrimination by the *Fatherland* toward soldiers of any campaign or any military unit who gave their lives in sacrifice for the sacred ideals of justice, freedom, and truth.

Let us respect suffering and death, but let us not dangerously confuse the young people who look to us, about good and evil, about truth and error, about the death of an aggressor and the death of his victim.

Let us say, if you will: we pray for those unfortunate people who have, through no fault of their own, been poisoned by a propaganda of hatred, and have sacrificed themselves for a misunderstood ideal of Fatherland, while unwittingly trampling underfoot every other noble human ideal.

Don Lorenzo Milani

NOTES

1. The Article continues: "... and as a means for settling international controversies."

2. The volunteer army of Garibaldi, acting on behalf of Victor Emmanuel I of the House of Savoy and King of Piedmont, completed his subjugation of the Bourbon Kingdom of the Two Sicilies by taking Naples. It was, up to that time, the largest territorial acquisition for Piedmont and for an eventually amalgamated Italy.

3. Here Milani is citing some of the remainder of Article 11 of the Constitution, which was to provide for eventualities such as the United Nations, the World Court, and the European Community. The entire Article reads as follows:

"Italy repudiates war as an instrument of aggression against the liberties of other peoples and as a means for settling international controversies; it agrees, on conditions of equality with other states, to such limitation of sovereignty as may be necessary for a system calculated to ensure peace and justice between nations; it promotes and encourages international organizations having such ends in view."

4. Before the third war of Italian unification, Italy signed a mutual aggression treaty with Bismarck's Prussia, the object being to seize the Veneto from Austria. Austria then offered through France to cede the Veneto if Italy would forgo the war. Italy, under General La Marmora, prime minister, refused the offer, with the hope of acquiring Trieste and the Trentino as well. The war proved to be a disaster for Italy. Austria kept Trieste and the Trentino, and ceded the Veneto (whose population failed to rise in Italy's behalf but who, after occupation by the Italian forces, accepted the cession by plebiscite).

5. This was the war against the Papal State to annex the remaining part of central Italy still under the Pope. France, which withdrew its troops from the protection of Rome, had been assured Italy would stand by the Convention of 1864, and that Rome was by international law inviolable. After a staged uprising failed to transpire, the Italian army seized Rome in 1870 and annexed the State.

6. National embarrassment abroad and agitation by socialist groups led to popular outcry for social reform. Mob rule and rampage occurred in Rome, Parma, Florence, and other cities. In Milan, after rioting led to the deaths of two policemen, General Fiorenzo Bava-Beccaris mistook a soup-line of beggars for rioters and turned cannon and grapeshot on them, killing eighty people and igniting four more days of street fighting. These events of May were on questionable evidence explained as a plot by socialist leaders who were, along with radicals and republicans, imprisoned. The universities of central Italy, the labor unions, the newspapers, the small banks, and about three thousand Catholic social organizations were shut down. Railway employees and civil servants were conscripted into the army so as to be under martial discipline and courts. The General's decoration was, to be exact, the Grand Cross of the Military Order of Savoy.

7. In order to take her place alongside other European imperialist powers, Italy created a colony, Eritrea, on the coast of the Red Sea, by sending a military expedition and bribing a local chieftain. When the forces moved further inland

into Abyssinia/Ethiopia, resistance followed, and a war ensued without any parliamentary oversight from Italy. Though costly in lire and lives, and offering no substantial economic advantage in Ethiopia, the war was continued in order to save face, to provide political success for an unstable government, and to strengthen the morale of the army (the only bulwark against lower-class unrest). Italy was defeated. Six thousand Italian soldiers lost their lives in the last battle— more Fallen in one day than in all the wars of the *Risorgimento* put together.

Fascist desire for an overseas empire led Mussolini to claim Abyssinia in order to propagate a virile race over the face of the earth, as he said. Peasant families were prevailed upon to follow the army as colonists: first into Libya and then into Ethiopia. British and French governments supported the Italian expansion in its early stages. After Addis Ababa had fallen, Mussolini expressed disappointment that only 1,537 Italians had been killed, for this meant that the army had been inadequately blooded and toughened. His son Vittorio published an account of the pleasure afforded by bombing village horsemen, who when hit would liquefy like a budding rose. Gas was used both during the invasion and during later uprisings. Ethiopia ended up costing ten times what it would return economically.

8. Giovanni Giolitti, who was to serve as prime minister in four governments between 1892 and 1921, eventually yielded to right-wing pressure for national expansion and manifest destiny and, having unsuccessfully sent a military mission to China in 1899–1900, he initiated a Libyan war in 1911–1912. He was opposed by the Turkish army (Libya had for centuries been part of the Ottoman Empire). Libyans, instead of turning against the Turks, fought valiantly against the invaders, whose frustration at the drawn-out and unsuccessful campaign led them to civilian slaughter and reprisals. Italy emerged from a very bloody war with title to Libya and the Dodecanese Islands, but in return paid what amounted to an indemnity to Turkey.

9. Cesare Battisti, as a young irredentist, had been prominent in Italian aspirations to annex the southern parts of Austria. In 1916 he was captured by the Austrians in the Veneto and, since he was Austrian by birth, was executed for treason.

10. The Triple Alliance (Prussia, Austro-Hungary, Italy) was three decades old when Giolitti, past his prime, renewed it a fourth time in 1912. As war with the Triple Entente (Great Britain, France, Russia) loomed, Giolitti was a neutralist but strong nationalism on left and right favored still more national expansion. Under his successor, Antonio Salandra, Italy negotiated with Germany and Austria for more territory, and after all five of the other powers were at war concessions were promised. Salandra then approached the Entente and concluded a secret treaty promising more Austrian and Ottoman territory in return for Italy's entry on their side. The Treaty of London was signed on 26 April 1915, and Italy renounced the Alliance on 4 May.

Meanwhile, to retain Italy as an ally, Austria offered the Trentino, the Sildtirol, and Trieste. Old patriot Gabriele D'Annunzio was sent round the major cities to stir up popular enthusiasm for war, because Salandra knew that national sentiment was then against entry into the conflict. Giolitti, who still controlled a majority in the Chamber of Deputies, which had been told nothing of these negotiations and which was against war, came back intending to reassume the prime ministry and to undo the recent commitments. Victor Emmanuel III, however, was bent on war, and supported D'Annunzio's demagoguery. Giolitti demurred, and backed away from marshalling his parliamentary supporters. The king reappointed Salandra, and during a parliamentary recess Italy sent its army to war on 24 May, less than three weeks after it broke the Alliance.

Milani's figures on Italian dead are a reasonable estimate. Financially, the war cost more than the sum of all Italian expenditures combined since its beginning in 1861. More than 500,000 Slavs and 200,000 German-speakers found themselves enclosed within her new borders.

11. Pius X (1903–1914), later canonized by Pius XII.

12. The elections of May 1921 gave the Fascists 35 seats in the Chamber of 535. Giolitti, once more premier, had helped them win even that many. Army and police troops had been told to ignore Fascist strong-arm intimidation across the land. A series of ineffectual cabinets yielded the nation to social chaos and violence. Mussolini's paramilitary blackshirts took over Ferrara, Milan, Parma, Pisa, and a host of other cities. Then, at the end of October 1922 the Fascists embarked upon a five-day March to Rome. The armed forces in many places were already fraternizing with the blackshirts. A caretaker government was asked to call out the army; they vacillated. Then in emergency session the cabinet drew up a martial-law decree, but the King refused to sign it. Two days later Mussolini had taken over the government. The general consensus is that the Italian military forces could easily have neutralized the Fascist bands if ordered to do so.

13. This is his estimate of the death toll of World War II, and perhaps of Mussolini's other armed ventures.

14. Italy sent as many as 70,000 troops for three years in aid of General Francisco Franco's rebellion in Spain. Army regulars eventually replaced the original blackshirts. Their performance was poor, and Mussolini's hope of acquiring the Balearic Islands was given no satisfaction.

15. When General Francisco Franco led the uprising of troops against the Republic in 1936, he claimed that the Socialist government was unlawful. Although the conservative parties had received a clear majority of the popular vote at the previous election, the arrangement of electoral districts produced a parliament in the hands of their opponents.

16. Five thousand Italians, led by Liberal Socialist Carlo Rosselli, Socialist Pietro Nenni, and Communist Luigi Longo, went to fight for the Spanish Republic. Many later fought as partisans in Italy in 1944–1945.

17. Milani omits to mention that Italy also declared war on and fought against Great Britain (1940) and the United States (1941).

18. Acts 5:29.

19. Concluded between Mussolini and Pius XI (1921–1939) on 11 February 1929, and commemorated on each anniversary. That holiday replaced one on 20 September, which had commemorated the seizure of Rome in 1870.

References

Burtchaell, J. T. (1988). *A just war no longer exists*. Notre Dame, IN: University of Notre Dame Press.

Coles, R. (1964). *Children of crisis*. Boston, MA: Atlantic Monthly Press.

Dennison, G. (1999). *The lives of children*. Portsmouth, NH: Boynton/Cook. (Original work published 1969)

Featherstone, J. (1971). *Schools where children learn*. New York: Liveright.

Goodman, P. (1962). *Utopian essays and practical proposals*. New York: Random House.

Graubard, A. (1972). *Free the children*. New York, NY: Pantheon Press.

Graves, D. (1988). When bad things happen to good ideas (audio cassette). Urbana, IL: National Council of Teachers of English.

Gutstein, E., & Peterson, B. (Eds.).(2005). *Rethinking mathematics*. Milwaukee, WI: Rethinking Schools.

Herndon, J. (1971). *How to survive in your native land*. New York: Bantam Books.

Hoffman, M. (1996). *Chasing hell hounds: A teacher learns from his students*. Minneapolis, MN: Milkweed Editions.

Joseph, S. M. (Ed.). (1969). *The me nobody knows: Children's voices from the ghetto*. New York: Avon.

King, Jr., M. L. (1967, April). *Beyond Vietnam: A time to break silence*. Speech delivered at Riverside Church, New York.

Kleindeinst, B. (Producer). (1994). *Farewell Barbiana* [Motion picture]. France: Cinema Guild.

Kohl, H. (1967). *36 children*. New York: New American Library.

Kozol, J. (1967). *Death at an early age*. New York: Penguin Books.

Kozol, J. (1992). *Savage inequalities*. New York: Harper Perennial.

Kozol, J. (2005). *Shame of the nation*. New York: Random House.

Menendez, R. (Director). (1988). *Stand and deliver* [Motion picture]. U.S. distributed by Warner Brothers.

O'Gorman, N. (1970). *The storefront*. New York: Harper Colophon.

Roderick, M., Nagoaka, J., & Allensworth, E. (2006). *From high school to the future: A first look at the Chicago public school graduate college enrollment, college preparation, and graduation from four-year colleges*. Consortium on Chicago School Research at the University of Chicago.

Rose, M. (1990). *Lives on the boundary*. New York: Penguin Books.

Schoolboys of Barbiana. (N. Rossi & T. Cole, Trans.). (1970). *Letter to a teacher*. New York: Random House.

Tomasi di Lampedusa, G. (1958). *Il gattopardo* [The leopard]. Milan: Feltrinelli.

About the Author

Marvin Hoffman has taught for more than 4 decades at many grade levels, from preschool to graduate school. His work has taken him to Mississippi, New York, Vermont, New Hampshire, Texas and, most recently, to Chicago, where he was the Founding Director of the North Kenwood Oakland Charter School. Currently he is the Associate Director of the Urban Teacher Education Program at the University of Chicago. His two previous books are *Vermont Diary* and *Chasing Hellhounds: A Teacher Learns from His Students.*

DATE DUE

GAYLORD

PRINTED IN U.S.A.